EXPLOSION
IN HALIFAX HARBOUR

THE ILLUSTRATED ACCOUNT OF A DISASTER THAT SHOOK THE WORLD

David B. Flemming

FORMAC PUBLISHING COMPANY LIMITED

HALIFAX

Formac Publishing Company Limited acknowledges the support of the Cultural Affairs Section, Nova Scotia Department of Tourism and Culture. We acknowledge the financial support of the Government of Canada through the Book Publishing Industry Development Program (BPIDP) for our publishing activities.

We acknowledge the support of the Canada Council for the Arts for our publishing program.

Library and Archives Canada Cataloguing in Publication

Flemming, David
    Explosion in Halifax Harbour : the illustrated account of a disaster
that shook the world / by David B. Flemmimg.

Includes index.
ISBN 0-88780-632-5

    1. Halifax (N.S.)--History--Explosion, 1917. 2. Halifax (N.S.)--History--Explosion, 1917--Pictorial works. I. Title.

FC2346.4.F57 2004   971.6'22503   C2004-904428-1

Formac Publishing Company Limited
5502 Atlantic Street
Halifax, Nova Scotia B3H 1G4
www.formac.ca

Printed and bound in Canada

This book is dedicated to Stella Marie Levy and William Bruce Flemming: Explosion survivors and my parents.

ACKNOWLEDGMENTS

Although my parents first sparked my interest in the Halifax Explosion as a young boy, over the years I have worked with others who have researched various aspects of the event. Among the many sources which I have drawn on, I want to acknowledge the following for their work and assistance over the years: John Griffith Armstrong, Blair Beed, Dan Conlin, Marilyn Gurney, Janet Kitz, Joan Payzant, Alan Ruffman, Joseph Scanlon, Garry Shutlak, and the CBC Archives.

A special thanks to Teresa Doré, and Sean, Mathew and Michael Flemming for their ongoing support.

Richmond and the Narrows as seen from the top of the grain elevator, c.1900. From lower right to upper left: the Intercolonial Railway yards, HMC Dockyard and the sugar refinery belching smoke. Note how the harbour narrows further north towards Bedford Basin.

Halifax was completed in 1854 with the Halifax terminus located in the area north of the Dockyard. Four large wooden piers were built in this northern suburb, which became known as Richmond, after the port in Virginia whence came much of the cotton destined for the textile mills of Canada or for transshipment abroad.

The Intercolonial Railway and the Dominion Government allocated $70,000 to build the new Deep Water Terminal to consist of three large piers near the corner of Upper Water and Cornwallis streets. Completed in 1880, it could accommodate the larger steamships which were calling at the port and was connected with the city's second railway line, the Intercolonial, which provided a direct service to markets in Quebec and Ontario. Deep Water was also the site of a major immigration facility and a grain elevator. The pier was refurbished prior to the outbreak of the First World War

Police constables with official staff car at Halifax Dockyard, 1917.

to accommodate the largest ocean liners afloat.

Throughout the 1880s and 1890s, Richmond became the location for the Halifax Graving Dock Company, the Acadia Sugar Refinery, the textile mill of the Halifax Cotton Company and the Grand Trunk Railway terminal, as well as a brewery, a large industrial foundry and a flour mill. These new industries attracted workers and their families to the neighbourhood. Churches of various denominations, schools and shops sprang up to meet the needs of the new inhabitants, turning what had been essentially a farming suburb into an important and populous part of the city. Further north, on the shores of Bedford Basin, was Africville, an African Nova Scotian community

The construction of the Halifax graving dock in 1885 provided the largest facility of its kind on the eastern seaboard. With its massive stonewalls and powerful pumps, it could accommodate all but the largest merchant or naval ships.

Family wedding at St. Mark's Anglican Church in the city's north end (1912).

which had been established in the 1840s.

Across the harbour, a brewery and a ropeworks opened in the less populated north end of Dartmouth, and together with the flourishing marine railways in Dartmouth Cove, they provided an industrial base for the town. A Mi'kmaq reserve at Turtle Grove, near Tufts Cove, immediately across the harbour from Richmond, was the last vestige of native settlement in what had been one of the earliest points of contact between Europeans and aboriginal peoples in Nova Scotia.

By the early twentieth century, the city's brief period of industrial development was beginning to wane. Although other eastern Canadian cities, such as Montreal and Toronto, had seen their populations grow by about 80 percent during the first decade of the century, Halifax's population grew by only 14 percent. Many Halifax industries were sold to larger central Canadian companies that would eventually move operations westward, leaving empty buildings and an unem-

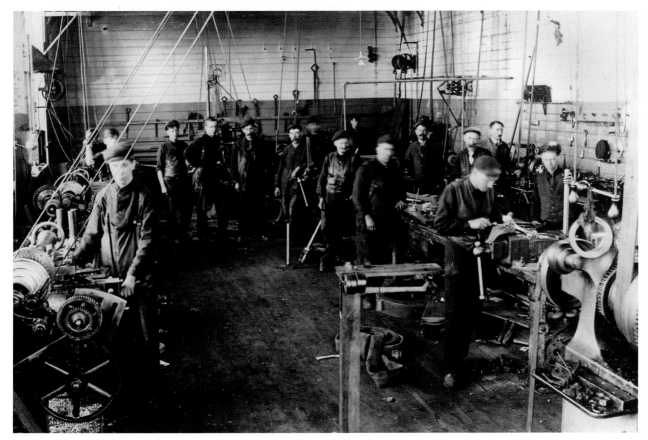

Machine shop at the Dockyard.

ployed work force in their wake. Many of these workers were to move to New England, more popularly known as the Boston States, to fill jobs in a rapidly growing industrial sector.

In an effort to make the port of Halifax "second to none on the continent of America" a major proposal to develop what was to become the Ocean Terminal in the South End of Halifax, consisting of 27 modern steamship berths, a large passenger and immigration facility and a grain elevator, was approved by the federal government in 1913. It was not possible to extend the existing rail lines south through downtown Halifax to link with the new facility, so the proposal included a new railway line that would be built along the west and south side of the peninsula. This involved cutting a bed for the railway, at some places 20 metres below grade, and expro-

priating land in the city's residential areas. Work on this massive project was well underway by 1914 but had slowed during the early years of the war.

Shipping tonnage had nearly doubled between 1913 and 1917, and the increase in marine traffic had taxed the resources of the port's infrastructure, including its human resources. Despite the recruitment of additional personnel, the harbour pilots worked long hours guiding the ships into and out of the harbour. The shipyard and Dockyard were both working at full clip and attracted new workers who had flocked to the city to share in the increased employment that the war offered. By 1917, the city's population had increased to 50,000 from its pre-war figure of 40,000.

The city was crowded with wartime workers, Canadian soldiers, naval personnel and merchant sailors.

Early sketch of proposed Ocean Terminals for Halifax, January 1910. This artist's rendering of an initial plan for the new port facilities bears only slight resemblance to what was actually built.

Sailors on shore leave added much to Halifax social life.

This influx of new people put a strain on the supply of adequate housing. The boarding houses were full, and by 1917 it was difficult for new arrivals to find accommodation for themselves and, in many cases, their families who had accompanied them. Besides the civilian workers, soldiers crowded the city streets, either preparing to embark for Europe, or manning the many military and defensive establishments in the area. Of the 5000 soldiers in Halifax in late 1917, more than 3000 were members of the Canadian Militia doing home defense duty. In addition, the Royal Canadian Naval College had a full complement of officers in training and other officers and ratings were either manning the naval vessels in port or undergoing training on board depot ships like HMCS *Niobe*.

The newspapers reflected a country at war. News accounts of battles at the front were interspersed with announcements

Two Royal Canadian Navy recruits in "square rig" and stokers' kit, 1910. The navy was established in 1910. These two trained in Halifax along with officer cadets, at the Royal Canadian Naval College. HMCS Niobe, *a former Royal Navy cruiser, was a depot ship moored at a Dockyard jetty at the time of the Explosion.*

drive, which ended on December 2, 1917, had succeeded in raising $300 million, twice what was asked. Triumphal returns of prominent Nova Scotians were touted as examples to potential recruits. The Royal Flying Corps was advertising for recruits "for immediate service." The National Hockey League was officially established in late November and the first games in the four-team league were scheduled for December 19. Haligonians, like all Canadians, were anticipating a new, temporary, wartime measure called "income tax." As it had been in times of conflict for over a century and a half, Halifax was again a wartime port, and it was anticipated that this time war would provide the city with a lasting legacy of economic development.

of war-related events and obituaries of victims of the conflict. Wounded soldiers disembarked at the Deep Water Terminals and were kept at the No. 6 Casualty Depot located at Pier 2. Many remained for a while at one of the city's hospitals before being sent home. Military medical authorities were anxiously awaiting the opening of the new military hospital at Camp Hill. Construction had recently been completed and furnishings and equipment had begun to arrive. These hospitals and their staff would soon make use of the skills learned from treating war casualties.

Haligonians were urged to purchase Victory Bonds to assist in the war effort and the bond

"Halifax Harbour in Time of War." A view of Halifax Harbour captured by Arthur Lismer, an official war artist.

2

DECEMBER 1917

Captain Aimé Le Médec probably felt a sense of relief as he saw the outer approaches of Halifax Harbour appear on the horizon on the afternoon of December 5, 1917. His vessel, *Mont-Blanc*, was four days out of New York and bound for Halifax, with her four holds and weather deck filled with over 2900 tonnes of explosives and flammable material including wet and dry picric acid, trinitrotoluene (TNT), gun cotton and benzene.

When she had been loaded in New York, the storage areas of the ship had been modified to prevent any friction that might cause a fire or subsequent explosion. The holds had been lined with wooden partitions and fastened with copper

A view of one of the last rowing clubs located on Halifax Harbour showing its proximity to the sugar refinery. Mont-Blanc *exploded less than half a kilometre north of the Lorne Rowing Club, destroying both it and the sugar refinery.*

By the outbreak of the First World War, steam ships had replaced the large sailing ships of the nineteenth century along the waterfront.

nails. The longshoremen who loaded the cargo had worn cotton socks over their shoes while walking on the metal decks.

Built in 1899 in Great Britain, *Mont-Blanc* was owned by la Compagnie Générale Transatlantique and registered in St-Nazaire, France. She was a single screw steamship of 2809 tonnes and 96 metres in length overall. Bound for Bordeaux, she was too slow to join the fast convoys from New York, travelling at 12-13 knots. She was ordered to Halifax to find a slower convoy more suitable for her speed of 7-8 knots. *Mont-Blanc* proceeded unescorted with only her 90 and 95 mm guns mounted fore and aft for protection. The voyage to Halifax was uneventful except for a bit of heavy weather, and by 1630 on Wednesday, December 5, *Mont-Blanc* reached the Examination Anchorage located just south of Mauger's Beach on the west side of McNabs Island where she took on Pilot Francis Mackey and awaited the

arrival of the Examining Officer.

In peacetime, vessels like *Mont-Blanc* embarked a pilot off Chebucto Head, and proceeded directly to a harbour anchorage or berth. In wartime, however, the responsibilities of the harbour-master were assigned to the Chief Examining Officer of the Royal Canadian Navy. The navy's Examination Service controlled all traffic in the harbour. It was the responsibility of the Examining Officer to check the ship's papers and cargo manifest prior to her proceeding through the outer and inner anti-submarine nets. These twin defensive works consisted of steel wire netting suspended from the surface to the harbour bottom along a long line held up by long wooden floats. A portion of the mid-section of the net could be opened as required by a "gate vessel." Two civilian tugs, *Nereid* and *Wilfred C*, were the assigned gate vessels. The outer gate was opened for an inbound vessel, and after the gate had been

Halifax Harbour from the Citadel, showing George's Island.

closed behind it, the inner net would be opened in a similar manner. A flotilla of minesweepers continually swept the outer approaches to the harbour, as far south as Chebucto Head. For security reasons, vessels were not permitted to pass through the net defences between dusk and dawn. Being late in the afternoon, Examining Officer Lieutenant Terrence Freeman informed *Mont-Blanc*'s captain and pilot that the vessel would have to remain at anchor until after sunrise on December 6.

Meanwhile, the Norwegian ship *Imo*, under charter to the Belgian Relief Commission, lay at anchor 10 kilometres to the north, near the western shore of Bedford Basin. *Imo* had arrived in Halifax on December 3, from Rotterdam, en route to New York to pick up relief supplies. Norway was a neutral country during the First World War and vessels like *Imo* car-

ried emergency supplies. As a non-combatant, she had the words "BELGIAN RELIEF" painted on her sides to deter attack from the warships. Neutral vessels were treated with some distrust, and they required naval and customs clearances both on arrival and prior to departure; their crews were not permitted to go ashore.

Imo had been cleared for departure at 1430 and had taken on Pilot William Hayes. A coal tender had been ordered to fill the ship's bunkers, but it arrived too late to permit the vessel to leave before the boom defense closed for the night. On his way home for the night, Pilot Hayes informed the pilotage office that *Imo* would remain at anchor until the morning of December 6.

Captain Haakon From, a Norwegian, led a primarily Scandinavian crew of 39. Captain From had been anxious

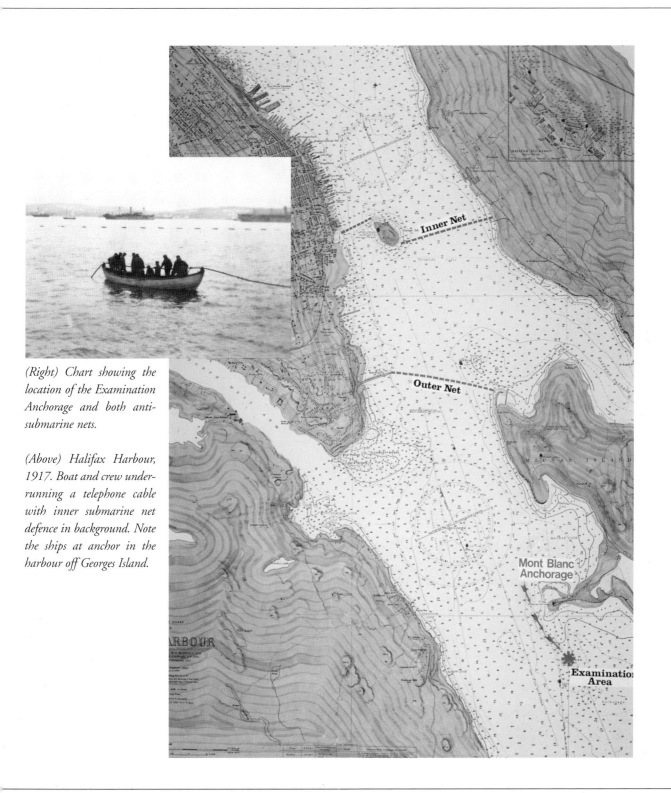

(Right) Chart showing the location of the Examination Anchorage and both anti-submarine nets.

(Above) Halifax Harbour, 1917. Boat and crew under-running a telephone cable with inner submarine net defence in background. Note the ships at anchor in the harbour off Georges Island.

the dry dock wharf undergoing repairs. The Norwegian vessel *Hovland* was in the dry dock, and as repairs on the British vessel *Middleham Castle* had just been completed, she was preparing to go to sea the following morning.

HMC Dockyard could not accommodate the large number of RCN vessels and other naval vessels in port. The Royal Canadian Navy had hoped to expand into the commercial waterfront of Richmond and had made plans to purchase the Atlantic Sugar Refinery, which was soon to be vacated, complete with 300 metres of wharf space. Other Canadian vessels either alongside the Dockyard jetties or at anchor in the harbour

The Canadian Garrison Artillery at Fort Charlotte, Georges Island, 1914. Many Haligonians volunteered for service in regiments like the Canadian Garrison Artillery. They saw service in defensive works that had been long unused, such as the Citadel, those on Georges Island, McNabs Island and York Redoubt.

to leave in the afternoon to allow his vessel to be well clear of the Nova Scotia coast, and any waiting enemy submarines, by the next morning.

The berths at the commercial wharves were full as usual. It was typical for vessels to wait at anchor for up to a week before gaining a berth to discharge or load their cargo. In Bedford Basin, nearly 40 ships were awaiting the departure of two convoys scheduled to leave on December 7 and 10. The Richmond piers were especially busy on December 5. The West Indies schooner *St. Bernard* was loading lumber at Pier 6 and the British vessels *Curaca* at Pier 8 and *Calonne* at Pier 9 were both loading horses. The British cargo vessel *Picton* had grounded off Halifax, and was at the sugar refinery wharf being unloaded in preparation to entering the dry dock. She carried a mixed cargo consisting of fused shells and grain. The USS *Old Colony* and the Canadian collier *J.A. McKee* were at

included the submarines *CC1* and *CC2*, auxiliary patrol ships HMCS *Cartier, Canada, Margaret* and *Hochelaga*; and numerous naval tugs, minesweeping trawlers, armed yachts and other motor boats. Many of the tugs and minesweepers were civilian ocean-going tugs or converted fishing seiners and many had civilian crews. The auxiliary patrol ship HMCS *Acadia*, a government survey ship in peacetime, served as a guard ship at the southeastern entrance to Bedford Basin opposite the Canadian Government Ship *Gulnare*. The cruiser HMCS *Niobe,* one of the first vessels acquired by the fledgling Royal Canadian Navy after its establishment in 1910, had been relegated to service as a depot ship and suffered the ignominy of having a wooden wall and roof built over her shelter deck making her look more like a houseboat than a once-proud ship of the line.

Other British and American naval vessels were also in port,

C. A. Mumford's was one of the few drugstores in Richmond. It was located on Barrington Street (formerly 49 Campbell Road), at the southeast corner of Barrington Street and East Young Street. The horse-drawn wagon, known as a sloven, was a familiar sight at most seaport towns of the time.

Intercolonial Railway Station and King Edward Hotel.

Arrival of Hospital Ship at Pier 2, c.1917, Arthur Lismer. Most of the troops departing Halifax for Europe or returning to Canada came through Pier 2. A military hospital was established here to act as a clearinghouse for the physically and emotionally wounded on their way to either a local hospital or points further west.

some undergoing repairs and others providing their crew with some welcome shore leave. Three British naval vessels, the armed merchant cruiser and escort ship HMS *Changuinola*, escort vessel HMS *Knight Templar* and the cruiser HMS *Highflyer,* were all anchored in the harbour off the Dockyard jetties. The United States Coast Guard patrol vessel *Morrill* was at anchor in Dartmouth Cove awaiting provisions.

The evening of December 5 was like any other during the war. The streets were crowded with civilians and military personnel; at home, students set to their homework after supper, and Haligonians stoked the fires for what promised to be a cold late autumn night. Blackout regulations had been in effect since late 1916 and after dusk the usually well-lit streets went dark as blinds and drapes were drawn.

After the coal tender discharged its cargo into *Imo's* bunkers, Captain From and his crew set about making final preparations for an early morning departure from *Imo's* anchorage in Bedford Basin. He had been assured by Pilot Hayes that he would be back onboard the vessel by 0700 the next morning.

Harbour Pilot Mackey decided to remain on board *Mont-Blanc* for the night. He shared a meal with Captain Le Médec in the wardroom and both looked forward to an early departure from the Examination Anchorage the next morning, Thursday, December 6.

Thursday morning reportedly dawned fair and cold with a temperature range of -6° to 2° C. By 0715, Le Médec had his vessel ready to weigh anchor. Mackey joined him on the

Mont-Blanc in Halifax Harbour, August 1900. This photo is from a scrapbook compiled by Joseph R. Bennett, a wharfinger and engineer with Pickford and Black, and possibly the ship's agent during this earlier visit. It appears that the vessel is coming alongside to load cargo. This image shows Mont-Blanc's upper rudder pintle, one of the largest pieces of the vessel to survive the explosion.

Mont-Blanc was built at Middleboro, England, in 1899 for La Compagnie Générale Transatlantique. Her gross tonnage was 3121 and her registered dimensions were length – 320 feet, breadth – 44.8 feet. She was powered by a single screw, 247 hp, triple expansion engine.

bridge and shortly before 0730 they received an order from the examination vessel to get underway. The American "tramp" steamer *Clara* preceded *Mont-Blanc* through the outer net defense which extended from the breakwater to the south of the Ocean Terminals, then under construction, across to Ives Point on McNabs Island. *Mont-Blanc* then continued through the inner net which ran from the north end of what is now Pier 20 to Georges Island, then across to the Dartmouth shore. She was making 6 - 7 knots but slowed to allow the Dartmouth ferry to pass and remained at a reduced speed of 4 knots as she steamed north towards the Narrows.

She approached HMS *Highflyer* on the starboard, or Dartmouth side, of the channel, saluting as she passed.

Shortly after 0800, Captain From weighed anchor and *Imo*, under the direction of Pilot Hayes, began to zig-zag its way through the seven or eight vessels at anchor in Bedford Basin, proceeding to the entrance to the Narrows. As *Imo* swung to starboard to enter the Narrows, Pilot Hayes noticed the American tramp, later identified as *Clara*, heading north along the Halifax shore, on the "wrong side" of the channel. Hayes ordered From to give two short blasts of *Imo's* steam whistle, indicating that she was directing her own course to

Originally built as a gunboat for the Royal Navy, by 1917 Stella Maris *was a commercial tug under charter to the Royal Canadian Navy. Captain Horatio Brannen and his crew were attempting to secure a line to the burning* Mont-Blanc *when the cargo exploded.*

port, to allow the American vessel to proceed into the Basin on her present course. After *Clara* passed into the Basin, a tug, *Stella Maris*, with two barges in tow, pulled away from Pier 8 causing *Imo* to maintain her course yet further towards the Dartmouth side of the channel.

At the about the same time, Pilot Mackey on the bridge of *Mont-Blanc* noticed the masts of a vessel entering the north end of the Narrows near Pier 9. When it appeared that the vessel was proceeding south, along the Dartmouth side of the channel, he ordered Le Médec to give one short blast of the ship's whistle signifying his intention to direct her course to starboard, closer to the Dartmouth shore. Since he had not heard a signal from the other vessel, *Imo*, and by being the first

to signal, Mackey and Le Médec laid claim to that side of the channel through which they were proceeding. Mackey slowed his vessel and *Imo* replied with two blasts of her whistle indicating that she was holding her course on the Dartmouth side of the channel so as to allow *Stella Maris* and her barges to proceed astern towards the east side of the Basin. Mackey reiterated his vessel's intention by repeating a single blast, to which Hayes repeated his intention with a further two blasts.

The two vessels were now heading on a collision course with neither indicating any intention of altering course. Mackey decided to turn his vessel to port so that both vessels would pass safely, starboard to starboard. Hayes replied with three blasts indicating his decision to put *Imo*'s engines in reverse. Since *Imo* was in ballast and was riding high in the water, it took a while for her twin screws to slow the vessel, and it forced her bow around to starboard. Mackey, believing that a collision was inevitable, ordered Le Médec to reverse her engines at full speed, hoping to lessen the effect.

The above sequence of events was described by Mackey and Le Médec. Their account differed slightly from the that of *Imo's* surviving witness, the helmsman Johan Johansen, who claimed that his vessel was closer to the middle of the channel than to the Dartmouth side and that the original two-whistle signal was directed at *Clara* and not at *Mont-Blanc*. Both Johansen and Edward Renner, *Clara's* pilot, claimed that *Mont-Blanc* and *Imo*

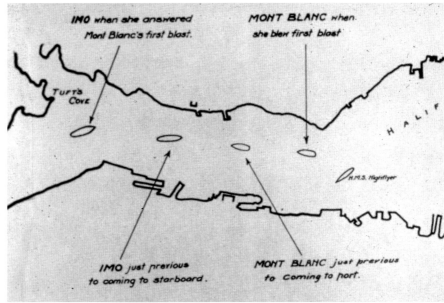

Course of Imo *and* Mont-Blanc *on entering the Narrows. Witnesses to the collision had conflicting views of the position of the ships in the channel, but it was apparent that the vessels were on a collision course.*

were two kilometres apart when the series of whistle signals began and not nearly as close as Mackey and Le Médec claimed. Johansen also claimed that after *Stella Maris* had passed astern of *Imo*, Pilot Hayes signalled one blast, indicating his intention to alter his vessel's course to starboard, bringing her closer to the Halifax side of the channel; he added that only after *Mont-Blanc* altered her course to port did *Imo* reverse her engines.

At approximately 0845, in either mid-channel or on the Halifax side of the channel, *Imo's* bow cut into the starboard bow of *Mont-Blanc* at nearly a right angle, near the No. 1 hold, making a two- to three-metre gash in her hull. The impact of the collision impeded the forward motion of *Imo*, allowing the propellers to quickly pull her away from the damaged *Mont-Blanc*. The friction of metal against metal sparked a fire in the picric acid that soon ignited the benzene spilling from some of the ruptured barrels stowed on deck. The fire and smoke spread with such rapidity that it was evident to Mackey and Le Médec that there would be no way to control the blaze. Le Médec ordered his crew to abandon

ship. They took to the lifeboats and began rowing towards the Dartmouth shore.

Although *Mont-Blanc's* engines had stopped, her momentum caused her to drift towards Pier 6 on the Halifax shore. Captain From turned *Imo* to port in an effort to move her away from the burning vessel and attempt to make her way back to the Basin. Within ten minutes of the collision, *Imo* lay perpendicular to both shorelines, nearly blocking the main channel.

The burning benzene poured onto *Mont-Blanc's* cargo of picric acid, gun cotton and TNT and began heating the full drums of fuel, causing a few to explode. Captain Horatio Brannen of *Stella Maris* ordered his crew to cast off the two barges and she steamed towards the burning ship, which had just nosed into the south side of Pier 6, spreading the flames to the wharf itself.

A seven-man whaler under the command of Captain T.K. Triggs was dispatched to the scene from HMS *Highflyer*. A steam pinnace from HMCS *Niobe* was also sent to assist in an effort to get a line aboard the burning ship and tow her away

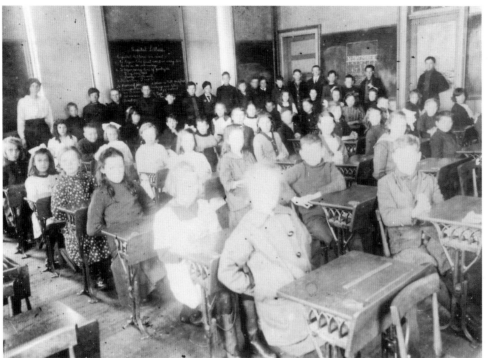

Grades 5 and 6, Richmond School, November 1916. Classrooms typically held as many as 70 students in several grades. It is likely that many of these children were among the 88 from the school who were killed in the explosion 11 months later.

Government Railway, yard and office workers and stevedores stopped and lined the outward rails of vessels to watch the smoke and flames and the occasional explosion of a shell or drum of benzene.

The numerous whistle signals, as well as the subsequent collision and fire, had attracted the attention of many on shore and on board other vessels in the harbour. Captain Mclaine of the tug *Douglas H. Thomas* had watched with concern as the ships approached each other but was relieved when it seemed as if they would pass starboard to starboard, avoiding a collision. Among the shipyard crew on board *Middleham Castle* was 18-year-old pipefitter Jack Tappen, who rushed to finish his work so he could join the other shipwrights at the rail watching the two vessels manoeuvring less than 200 metres away.

from the pier. Lieutenant Commander James Murray, transport officer with the Port Convoy Office, was on board the tug *Hilford* coming out of the Basin. Murray knew of *Mont-Blanc's* cargo and he came ashore to call for assistance in fighting the fire.

Triggs and his crew attempted to secure a hawser to the burning ship so that *Stella Maris* could tow her back to the middle of the harbour. *Mont-Blanc's* bow came ashore on the south side of Pier 6 and more than two-thirds of the length of the pier was now exposed to the ever-increasing inferno. Several efforts to move the vessel had failed, when Captain Brannen ordered his son Walter to play out a larger line from *Stella Maris's* hold. Other members of the crew used her pump and hoses to spray water over both the burning ship and the pier.

After the collision, work ceased around the harbour. At the shipyard, at the Richmond piers and the Canadian

Richmond School was located a few blocks west of Pier 6, and since classes didn't start until 0930 many of the students made a detour on their route to school to get closer to the action, or left home early to watch the excitement in the harbour. Noble Driscoll lived on Barrington Street (known as Campbell Road until 1919), overlooking the Narrows. He and his brother Gordon were ardent harbour watchers and delighted in identifying the various types of vessels, even drawing them in their school scribblers. As he was getting ready for school he heard the ships' signals and saw the collision and ensuing fire. He and Gordon ran towards Pier 6 and stood near a bridge over the railway track to watch the burning ship. Thirteen-year-old James Pattison and his older brother Gordon left their house on Barrington Street, running along-

Grade 3 class at Richmond School, 1916-17.

side the fire truck as it raced past the Protestant orphanage.

St. Joseph's Boys' School had been destroyed by a fire in 1916 resulting in St. Joseph's Girls' School providing classes for girls in the morning and boys in the afternoon. Minnie (Mary) Anderson, a first-grade student who lived on Livingstone Street, arrived at school a few minutes before nine o'clock where she rushed to the cloakroom so as not to be late for morning prayers. Eileen Ryan, 10 years old, was going to the basement cloakroom when she heard the fire engine *Patricia* speeding up Gottingen Street towards Fort Needham. She went to her desk in their makeshift classroom on the stage of the auditorium and placed the apple she was saving

Home of Vincent Pattison and his family, 1263 Barrington Street, c.1910. Pattison worked at the Atlantic Sugar Refinery, less than three blocks north of his home.

for recess in her desk.

When it was apparent that the flames from *Mont-Blanc* were threatening the pier, Constance (Con) Upham, whose grocery store was located on Barrington Street opposite Pier 6, sounded the alarm from a nearby fire alarm box. It was not uncommon for firefighters to respond to alarms from Box No. 83. It was located close to the shipyard and the Richmond Terminal, where small fires aboard ships or on the docks were a common occurrence. The motor pumper *Patricia* was the first fire apparatus to arrive in response to the

alarm. Close behind was a car carrying Chief Edward Condon and Deputy Chief William Brunt. *Patricia's* crew began to roll out the hose and attach it to a nearby hydrant. Condon, assessing the seriousness of the situation, issued a general alarm for apparatus from all the city's fire stations to rush to the scene.

Upham and his staff went outside to watch the fire, while urging many of the onlookers not to venture too close to the wharf. He was joined by Jack Ronayne, a reporter from the *Halifax Echo*, who arrived soon after the firemen and began

Richmond railway terminal and yards with Pier 6 in the foreground, viewed from the roof of the sugar refinery, c. 1900.

working his way through the crowd towards Pier 6. Con's brother Martin lingered awhile and then set off up Kaye Street to begin his grocery deliveries.

The staff at the Hillis and Sons Foundry, located just up the hill, had a good view of the fire. Hillis employed nearly 80 workers and most of them soon drifted from their work to line the foundry windows to watch the burning ship. A young apprentice, Frank Burford, was ordered away from the window to make an urgent delivery to the graving dock. He ran down the hill at a fast clip so as not to miss any of the excitement. Another foundry worker, who had gone down the

hill to get a better look, became frightened as the fused shells began to explode and turned around, running back up the hill towards the foundry.

William Lovett, the chief clerk at the Richmond railway yard, called his boss at the Canadian Government Railway office to inform him that a munitions ship was on fire and there was a danger that it could explode. Lovett and the train dispatcher, Vincent Coleman, were fleeing the office when Coleman decided to return to telegraph a warning to an inbound train: "Munitions ship on fire. Making for Pier 6. Goodbye." John Hinch, a shunter man at the Canadian

Kaye Street Methodist Church was built in 1868. It was enlarged, with the addition of a hall five years later. In December 1917, Rev. William Swetnam, his wife and two children lived on East Young Street.

remained on top to continue watching.

Many women in homes overlooking the harbour stood at windows with their children or bundled them up and stood on porches and in yards to watch the fire as black smoke billowed high into the clear sky. Eric Davidson's mother held her two-and-a-half-year-old son on her lap as she explained to him what has happening in the harbour. Eric was less interested in the burning ship than he was in running his toy car along the window sill.

The large column of gray-black smoke was rent occasionally by balls of flame from exploding drums of benzene or from the exploding shells. Captivated by the scene, teenagers Barbara Orr and her brother Ian rushed from their house, across Mulgrave Park, towards the waterfront. At their home on East Young Street, the family of Rev. William Swetnam, the pastor at Kaye Street Methodist Church, had just finished breakfast. All had gathered around the piano to listen to wife and mother Elizabeth accompany eight-year-old Carman, who was scheduled to sing at a mission band concert that evening at the church. Six-year-old Dorothy sat in an armchair while the pastor stood by the entrance to the parlour waiting for Carman to begin singing.

In other parts of the city, people also went about their reg-

Government Railway's Richmond yards, and a friend climbed on the top of a boxcar to watch the flames. They saw *Patricia* racing towards Pier 6, however, the exploding shells made Hinch fear for his safety and he started down the ladder on the side of the boxcar away from the burning ship. His friend

Built in 1872 and enlarged in 1894, Grove Presbyterian Church was located just up the hill from Richmond School. Rev. Charles Crowdis, lived in the manse on Gottingen Street with his wife and two children.

ular business. Frank Willis was on his way to Tower Road School when he and a friend stopped at Doody's Candy Store at the corner of Bland Street and Victoria Road to view the sweets displayed in the store window. Nine-year-old Bill Carter had just hung up his coat at Oxford Street School and was kneeling at his desk to begin morning prayers.

Evelyn Richardson took the early "suburban" train from Bedford with her father on the morning of December 6. Together they walked from North Street Station to Alexandra School, where her father was the principal. Then Evelyn con-

tinued south to Halifax County Academy where she joined her fellow students and teachers for a hymn and prayers in the school's assembly hall. As prayers commenced she noticed the clear blue sky through the north-facing window.

In Dartmouth, school began at 0900. Most students, like 13-year-old Norman Moir, were taking their seats in class after having hung up their outer clothing in the cloakrooms. Mollie Brazier was in Grade 9 at Greenvale School but was at home on the morning of the sixth. Her younger brother saw *Mont-Blanc* burning and Molly and a friend went down to

The cloud of smoke as seen from Elmsdale, over 40 kilometres from the blast.

Above: This photo of the cloud was probably taken from a ship near the Examination Anchorage with Point Pleasant in the background. The vessel in the foreground resembles an ocean-going tug.

Right: This photo was taken by a soldier stationed at York Redoubt, a defensive fortification located at the outer approaches to Halifax Harbour.

Windmill Road to watch. Owen Sawlor stopped at the foot of Dawson Street on his way to Park School and had a clear view to the harbour. At the Halifax Brewery in Turtle Grove, workers gathered outside to watch the exploding shells and barrels of benzene.

One of the best viewpoints of the action was from a small grove of spruce on the Mi'kmaq reserve at Tufts Cove. Families wandered down to the shore to get a better view of the burning ship. Also on the eastern shore near Tufts Cove, Nellie Flynn, who lived with her aunt and uncle, was alerted to the fire by the noise. While she was looking out the window, she saw a group of men running up from the shore. Although they were strangers and seemed to be dressed differently, she and her aunt recognized one of them as Francis Mackey, an acquaintance of her uncle.

The dense column of smoke, which reached heights of up to 60 metres, was rent

*One of the many photos taken of the smoke cloud.
(Opposite) The north face of the City Hall clock stopped at 0905 and sits today always at this time as a memorial to the Explosion.*

by at least four columns of flame caused by the admixture of gasoline vapours and the oxygen in the air. Shortly before 0905, *Mont-Blanc*'s cargo exploded in one massive blast. *Mont-Blanc* disintegrated in an instant, hurling thousands of fragments of hot steel enveloped in a black oily substance up along the Halifax and Dartmouth sides of the harbour, razing everything and everyone in its wake. A large cloud of billowing, greyish-white smoke cut through the black smoke caused by the pre-explosion fire and soared

upwards over 3600 metres.

The magnitude and significance of the Halifax Explosion is illustrated in its having been carefully studied by a group of scientists who convened at the University of California at Berkeley to consider the use of the newly developed atomic bomb. In an effort to predict the effect of such a weapon, they studied the effect of other explosions, including the explosion of *Mont-Blanc*. Many had occurred on ships at sea or in relatively isolated areas, but what made the Halifax blast of particular interest was that it occurred in an urban setting. The new proposed bomb was to be an "air burst" and not a "ground burst," such as the Halifax Explosion. They estimated that if the Halifax Explosion had occurred at a distance above ground, the overall destruction and loss of life would have been much worse. The first atomic bomb, known as the Trinity test blast, was the equivalent of 19 kilotons of TNT, compared to just under three kilotons for the explosion at Halifax. The bombs detonated over Hiroshima and Nagasaki (13 and 23 kilotons respectively) were also significantly larger than the Halifax blast, and it is therefore not surprising that they wrought more widespread devastation.

Nevertheless, the Explosion at Halifax on December 6, 1917 was probably the most significant explosion, given the size and location, that they could study.

3

DEVASTATION, DEATH AND SURVIVAL

Many of the survivors of that day mention experiencing a silence as the explosion occurred. Some felt an immense pressure on their bodies and many were thrown a great distance by the concussion. Others describe a deafening noise followed by silence and darkness. Naval divers who were underwater at the time of the explosion recount seeing most of the water in the harbour displaced as the shock wave from the blast, like a tsunami, seemed to push it away from the site of the blast.

Pier 6 and the wooden schooner *St. Bernard* alongside disappeared with nary a trace. The other three Richmond piers were all but destroyed.

The American Naval cruiser USS *Tacoma* felt the concussion from the blast 80 kilometres out to sea as did the armed troop transport USS *Von Steuben*. Both immediately altered course to Halifax to assist with the rescue efforts. Captain W.M.A. Campbell of the Canadian merchant ship *Acadian*, which was inward bound, 28 kilometres to seaward, felt the concussion from the blast and used his sextant to measure the column of smoke rising 3600 metres high above the city. He noted that two "angry looking flames of fire" initially shot up higher than the cloud of smoke itself.

View of HALIFAX N.S. after disaster Dec. 6, 1917 LOOKING SOUTH

(Right) Ira McNab's Clock.
Recovered from a ruined house in Richmond, it is now part of the history collection at the Nova Scotia Museum.

(Below) Panoramic view looking south towards the graving dock and HMC Dockyard. From left to right: ruins of the Halifax Graving Dock Company's machine shop; SS Hovland *in the drydock, shorn of her superstructure; the railway tracks stretching south to the remains of North Street Station; and the ruins of many homes and businesses. HMS* Highflyer *is anchored in the harbour and HMCS* Niobe *is alongside a Dockyard jetty beneath the black smoke. Despite the damage and chaos, the routine in the port was disrupted only slightly. A convoy of 33 ships, escorted by* Highflyer, *left Halifax for Europe on December 11, only four days after its scheduled departure date.*

St. Joseph's Convent, located on the southeast corner of Gottingen and Kaye streets, was home to the Sisters of Charity who taught at St. Joseph's Boys' and Girls' Schools. The wrecked building was demolished and by 1920 a new St. Joseph's Church was built on the site.

The explosion caused a ground, or seismic, wave and an air, or shock, wave. The ground wave travelled twenty times faster than the air wave, explaining the numerous accounts of two explosions at various intervals. The low frequency

Piece of hull plating from Mont-Blanc. *The force and heat from the explosion resulted in the twisting of the steel plates.*

sounds, known as infrasound, were detected nearly 300 kilometres away, with many accounts of what seemed like two or three explosions being detected. Because the sound waves bent upwards before bending back to earth, the Explosion was detected in some areas hundreds of kilometres away, but not in others less than 100 kilometres from the blast site. The shock wave broke windows as far away as Truro, at a distance of 80 kilometres.

Few structures within 500 metres of the blast were left standing, and the remnants of those that remained were damaged beyond repair, as the shock wave from the blast swept the debris from the buildings along the ground, eastward on the Dartmouth side of the harbour and westward to the summit of Fort Needham and beyond. Fires from the blast or from overturned stoves broke out among the ruins, and were fed by the splintered wood and oily soot. In the area between East Young Street on the south, the harbour on the east, Fort Needham to the west and Rector Street to the north, none of the buildings remained. The damage beyond these boundaries was severe though many buildings that did not collapse or burn were repairable. Soldiers who had served in France remarked that the square mile of Richmond adjacent to Pier 6 looked worse than any of the devastation that they had seen in Flanders.

Of the vessels which came to the aid of the burning *Mont-Blanc*, the entire six-man crew of *Niobe*'s whaler were killed and only Able Seaman William Becker of the five-member crew of *Highflyer*'s steam pinnace survived. On board *Stella Maris*, Walter Brannen survived by being hurled into the hold while trying to reach a tow line being played out by a crew member below deck. Only five members of *Stella Maris*'s crew of 24 survived. There were 25 RCN personnel killed in the explosion, 17 of which were members of *Niobe*'s crew.

Eight members of the RCN and RN were decorated for their actions during the period of the disaster.

Cdr. T.K. Triggs, RN, was given the Albert Medal-Gold for his actions as commander of

SS Calonne *at Pier 8. Most of the ship's crew and the stevedores who gathered at her stern were killed instantly by the blast. On the left is the stern of the tug* Hilford *that was tossed out of the water and onto the pier.*

Highflyer's whaler crew. The Albert Medal-Bronze decoration was awarded to five members of the RCN and RN; only ABS William Becker survived to receive his award. Chief Master of Arms, John Gammon of HMCS *Niobe*, who had saved the navy divers, was made a member of the Order of the British Empire. Another RN rating, W.S. Critch, killed in the blast, received the Meritorious Service Medal.

The body of Vincent Coleman was found near the Canadian Government Railway office where he had returned to telegraph a warning to the incoming train. John Hinch, whose concern about the burning ship prompted him to climb down

Urged to leave his post at the Canadian Government Railway Office, Vincent Coleman chose to remain so he could telegraph a warning to an incoming train at Rockingham. The train stopped and some of the passengers had begun the long walk to Halifax, when SS Mont-Blanc *exploded. Coleman's body was found with a piece of his telegraph key nearby.*

SS Curaca *was blown from her berth at Pier 8, across the Narrows and onto the Dartmouth shore, with the loss of over 40 of her crew. She was later refloated and repaired.*

from the top of the boxcar, survived by being blown between two railway cars. He sustained a shrapnel wound to one eye, which required its removal. His friend was blown off the top of the car on which he was standing, and perished.

The Acadia Sugar Refinery, once considered "the tallest building east of Montreal," was reduced to an unrecognizable heap of rubble, entombing over 20 workers, most of who had been watching the burning *Mont-Blanc* from the roof of the building. Over 120 men working in and about the dry dock were killed and others had to be rescued after being

Armed cruiser HMS Calgarian *at anchor after the Explosion. The hull is painted in a "dazzle" design to camouflage the vessel while at sea by making its profile blend in with the sky and ocean when seen from the periscope of an enemy submarine or from the air.*

Coastal drifter CD74 and the damaged torpedo shops. A similar vessel, CD73, was badly damaged by the explosion while her crew watched the efforts to tow the burning Mont-Blanc *away from Pier 6.*

Top: *Even though it was located over two kilometres to the west of the blast, the roundhouse and other railway repair sheds suffered extensive damage.*

Right: *The Dominion Textile Mill collapsed trapping many of the workers amidst a tangle of debris and machinery. Only the chimney survived the blast.*

The pile of rubble marks the former location of the Acadia Sugar Refinery. To its right is the shell of the shipyard machine shop. On the Dartmouth shore of the harbour is the French Cable Wharf and cable building (left), built in 1916. Both survived the blast.

Right: The current view to the east from the top of Fort Needham looking across the harbour stands in stark contrast to the view as seen a few days after the explosion.

This solitary house located on the north side of Duffus Street near Gottingen Street, reflects both the power of the explosion and the house's resilience. It can be seen standing defiant in many photographs of the area taken immediately following the explosion.

swept into the harbour. The Naval College, located less than two kilometres from Pier 6, was badly damaged and while few cadets or staff were killed, many suffered horrible wounds. A number of the senior cadets had been watching the fire when the large front window exploded in upon them, resulting in many serious eye injuries.

Apart from *Mont-Blanc* and *Imo,* the ships close to the site of the explosion suffered devastation and great loss of life. Many who would ordinarily have been below deck had joined their shipmates or longshoremen on weather decks to watch the fire. *Calonne* and *Curaca,* located at Piers 8 and 9, lost over 60 crew members. Edward Crossman, one of the few survivors from *Curaca*, had left his shipmates on deck watching the fire to go below for a cigarette: a cigarette that saved his life.

Over 50 of the longshoremen unloading *Picton*'s cargo perished in a matter of minutes. These brave men had been busy securing *Picton*'s cargo holds full of explosives in anticipation of the fire from *Mont-Blanc*

spreading along the shoreline to where she was alongside at the Graving Dock. For many of these victims, the coroner's report states "body not recovered" or "reported missing." Jack Tappen was hurled down a companionway on *Middleham Castle* and, although shaken up, was not injured. With some difficulty, he managed to get ashore with other members of the ship's crew, where they rescued numerous people trapped in nearby houses.

Fort Needham hill protected the buildings below its western slope by deflecting the blast upwards and to the west, where its force unfortunately came crashing down with devastating effect. The Dominion Textile Company's cotton factory, where the roof and the second floor collapsed, entombed dozens of workers under a mass of cement and broken machinery.

Other large buildings including the Provincial Exhibition Building, the Nova Scotia Car Works and the Canadian

Portion of the upper rudder pintle from SS Mont-Blanc. *This solid piece of steel weighs 300 kilograms and was found over two kilometres from the site of the explosion.*

Imo *ashore at Dartmouth. After the collision,* Imo's *captain had attempted to bring the vessel about to return to Bedford Basin. The explosion blew the vessel ashore just south of the French Cable Wharf. Her funnel and superstructure were badly damaged and the hull was riddled with shrapnel.* Imo *was built by Harland and Wolff at Belfast in 1889. She was named* Runic *and later* Tampican *before assuming the name* Imo *in 1912 when owned by the South Pacific Whaling Company. She was 5043 gross tons and her registered dimensions were length – 430 feet, breadth – 45 feet. She was driven by a 424 hp, single screw, triple expansion steam engine.*

Government Railway roundhouse were badly damaged, often left beyond repair. Many buildings west of Gottingen Street suffered structural damage resulting from the vacuum created by the force of the blast. The lack of air pressure outside provided no resistance to the internal air pressure of the buildings, causing the walls to buckle outward.

Of the four schools only the newly built Alexander McKay School survived, bearing just moderate damage. Most of the 189 students who lost their lives in the Explosion were either on their way to school or, in the case of St. Joseph's School students, had just begun religious instruction. All four Richmond churches were destroyed. Together, the four parishes — St. Joseph's, St. Mark's, Grove Presbyterian and Kaye Street Methodist — later estimated that over 840 of their parishioners perished in the blast.

Richmond School, c.1915. (Sometimes referred to as Roome Street School.) By 1917 more than 400 students were being taught by just seven teachers. School did not start until 0930, and by 0905 only a few students were in the schoolyard. Many had rushed down to the waterfront to watch the burning ship. A total of 88 Richmond School students lost their lives in the explosion. A plaque bearing their names was mounted in the new Richmond School, now the Nova Scotia Family Court.

St. Joseph's Parish Hall. Many buildings suffered similar damage from the bowing out of exterior walls. This building was repaired and was still in use 86 years after the Explosion as a commercial building.

Halifax Fire Department pumper Patricia was the first motorized pumper used in Canada. It was damaged in the Explosion but after being repaired, remained in service until 1942.

Pilot Mackey, Captain Le Médec and the crew of *Mont-Blanc* had taken cover in a Dartmouth field just south of the Halifax Brewery at Turtle Grove. Some of them suffered minor injuries and the one crew member who was severely injured subsequently died. The crew were making their way towards Dartmouth when they were rescued by a naval launch which brought them to Halifax where they were placed under an armed guard.

Imo ended up aground on the Dartmouth shore, with her superstructure laid clean. She lost six of her crew including Captain From, whose body was later recovered near the ruins of the Halifax Brewery on the Dartmouth shore. Pilot Hayes's lifeless body was later recovered on Brunswick Street. The only member of the deck crew to survive was the helmsman, Johan

Johansen. He and the other crew members were subsequently rescued from their grounded ship and taken to Halifax.

Of the children on their way to school, Noble Driscoll was hurled through the air by the Explosion, landing over half a kilometre from where he had been watching the burning *Mont-Blanc*. When he regained consciousness, just behind the ruins of Richmond School, he discovered his coat and hat were missing and Gordon was nowhere to be found. He made his way back home where he found most of his family. The family were sent to Truro by train where they were cared for until another more permanent home was found. Gordon Driscoll's body was never recovered.

Frank Willis had still been looking at the candy in the store window when he heard a loud noise and the concussion

Oland Brewery, Agricola Street, Halifax. A new brewery, rebuilt on the same site in the 1920s, continues to operate under the Oland name.

knocked him off his feet. At first he thought the blast was just another explosion connected with the construction of the new railway cut. Noise from these blasts had become commonplace in the South End of the city, however he had never experienced one which caused such an air wave. Mrs. Doody, the proprietor of the candy shop, suffered lacerations when the store window blew in but Frank and his friend Peter were unhurt.

James Pattison recalled a strange silence before awaking entangled in trolley wires. His nose was bleeding and a piece of metal was embedded in his hand. His leather school bag had been ripped by a piece of shrapnel and he had lost his

jacket. He found his brother, Gordon, and they went back to their house, which they found in flames. Their siblings Alan and Katherine died at home and their father's body was found amidst the ruins of the sugar refinery four months later.

Bill Carter's school prayers had just begun when the blast occurred. The window he was facing blew in, cutting his eyebrows and head. He went home to his parents and was taken to hospital where slivers of glass were removed from his forehead. Seventy-five year later, Bill was still retrieving pieces of glass from his scalp and eyebrows. He thanked his morning prayers for saving his life, feeling that in all likelihood he would have been killed had he been standing or sitting facing the window, rather than kneeling as he had been.

At St. Joseph's School, the top floor collapsed onto the one below, trapping many students in a jumble of wood and plaster. Minnie Anderson's face was cut and one of her eyes was badly injured from the shattered glass of the cloakroom

Remains of the Richmond piers. A small tug alongside the wreck of Stella Maris, *the tug that was trying to tow* Mont-Blanc *away from Pier 6. The foot of Pier 6 can be seen to the left of the wreck and Piers 7, 8 and 9 are in the background.* Stella Maris *was eventually refloated and repaired and she continued in service for another decade.*

window. She and her sister made their way home where their mother bandaged their injuries and took them to the hospital. Eileen Ryan, the girl who had carefully placed her apple in her desk, drifted in and out of consciousness. Her cuts and bruises masked the pain from a broken collarbone and a dislocated shoulder. She eventually found her way along Macara Street to her home, where she was reunited with her family then taken to the hospital.

Evelyn Richardson, standing at a distance, saw the north-facing school window shatter on the students and teachers of the Halifax Academy. Uninjured, she eventually made her way to Brunswick Street where she met her father; together they returned to their home in Bedford.

The body of Con Upham, the man who had raised the fire alarm, was never recovered. Martin, Con's brother, who had left to deliver the groceries, survived to rescue his two children from their collapsed house. He was, however, unable to rescue his wife from the rubble.

Jack Ronayne, the reporter who was last seen talking to Upham, was killed instantly.

In all, 13 fire apparatus responded to the two alarms for assistance. Besides the chief and deputy chief, seven other firefighters perished in the blast, including the entire crew of *Patricia,* except for the driver, Billy Wells, who sustained serious injuries.

Many people were killed or injured at or near their homes.

Ruins of Richmond Terminal and wharves can be seen in the foreground. The wreck of the naval tug Hilford *can be seen at far right on her side atop Pier 8.*

Eric Davidson was blinded by the exploding glass from the window, the sill of which had been, seconds before, a road for his toy fire engine. His mother received severe cuts to her neck and face but managed get Eric and her daughter Marjorie to safety. Barbara Orr was blown half a kilometre to the top of Fort Needham, losing one of her high-laced boots in the process. She was unable to find her brother Ian and when she returned to her house on Kenny Street, she found it engulfed in flames. She walked to her aunt's house and was treated for

her injuries. Her worst fears were realized in the following days when she discovered that her mother, father, three brothers and two sisters — her entire immediate family — had died.

Reverend William Swetnam suffered only minor injuries as his house collapsed in flames around him. His wife and son, who had been rehearsing at the piano, disappeared beneath a pile of burning rubble. With the help of neighbours, he was able to rescue his daughter Dorothy just in time to prevent her being burned to death. Workers searching through the rubble

The area north of the Hillis & Son Foundry towards Pier 8 was a scene of total desolation and destruction.

a few weeks later discovered a few human bones in the basement underneath metal remnants of the piano.

Near the foundry, Frank Burford, who had run down the hill to make a delivery, awoke to find himself buried under a pile of timbers and plaster. Though he suffered numerous cuts and bruises and a serious leg injury, he was one of the more fortunate of Hillis Foundry employees; over 40 workers perished there, including his father, whose name he bore.

All along the Dartmouth shore, buildings collapsed or had windows shattered. Mollie Brazier, who had been watching the burning ship from Windmill Road, was knocked down by the explosion and saw a huge tidal wave come up the harbour with what she thought was a tugboat on top of it. She has-

tened home and helped rescue her mother and brother from the wreckage of their house.

Edith Murphy and her mother sought safety for themselves and her two-year-old sister. The horrible suffering that Edith witnessed included the sight of a man impaled on a fence with his life draining away.

Owen Sawler never did get to school that morning. He remembered feeling the concussion from the blast and soot and steel raining down from the sky. He barely escaped injury when the chimney of Emmanuel Church collapsed. Returning home, he found his mother and brother uninjured.

Near Tufts Cove, Nellie Flynn and her aunt dug their way out of the rubble of their house and hid in the well, fearing

Looking south from Wellington Barracks at the destruction of the Dockyard. USS Old Colony, a former passenger vessel which had stopped in Halifax for repairs is docked at the naval coaling wharf. Her crew undertook some of the first rescue efforts and the vessel served as a hospital, providing medical care and hot meals for the injured as well as for the rescue personnel.

another "German attack." Her uncle came home, then took them to safety, on the way encountering a blind woman who was seeking directions to the harbour, where she planned to drown herself.

Halifax Breweries at Turtle Grove was totally destroyed and seven of its employees were killed, including the manager, Conrad Oland, and William Dumaresq. Dumaresq's wife and daughter were both blinded at their home in Tufts Cove.

At the Mi'kmaq reserve at Tufts Cove, nine of the 21 residents perished. The survivors were moved to other reserves. The school and all of the homes were destroyed. The village was never rebuilt.

Throughout the whole ordeal, the Dartmouth ferries continued to operate, enabling survivors to help loved ones or to find shelter.

The community of Africville, located just beyond the Narrows on the south side of Bedford Basin, suffered minor damage, although three of its inhabitants were killed, likely while working in Richmond.

Within minutes of the blast, the entire community of Richmond lay in ruins and other parts of the north ends of Halifax and Dartmouth suffered extensive damage. Areas of Halifax south of North Street had extensive damage from broken windows and collapsed roofs. Most of the deaths occurred within two kilometres of the blast. In other parts of the city, people suffered terrible wounds from flying shrapnel. Amidst the devastation, survivors soon overcame the initial shock of the explosion and their efforts quickly turned to tending to their injuries, reuniting with their families and helping their friends and neighbours.

4

RESCUE AND RECOVERY

escue efforts began within minutes of the explosion. Many who were uninjured immediately turned to care for their families or those around them. Most people who were not with their families tried to return home as quickly as possible. This was especially true with school children. Efforts to save those trapped in burning houses met with limited success. There were many demands on too few people, especially within the immediate area of destruction.

The house on the left was damaged when the normal interior air pressure pushed outward against the walls at the same time that a vacuum was created outside by the air forced by the blast. Many other homes in this area were repaired and were still standing nearly nine decades later.

Soldiers searching through remnants of houses near Mulgrave Park.

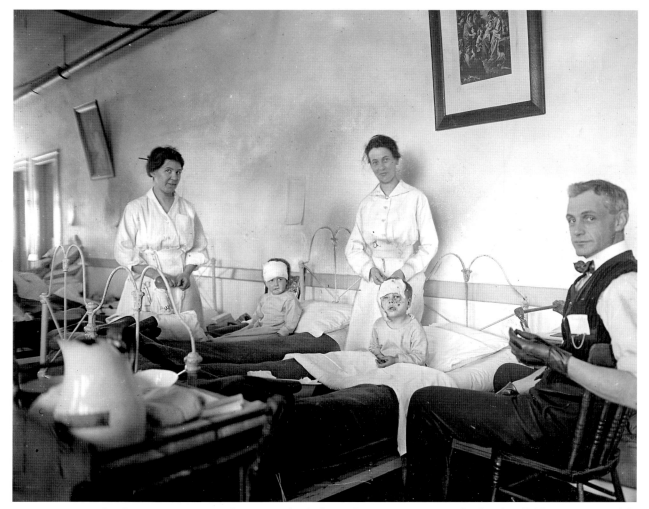

Patients, nurses and a doctor at St. Mary's College Hospital. The hospital at St. Mary's was outfitted and staffed by Unit No. 5 of the Massachusetts Halifax Relief Committee and the American Red Cross, commanded by Dr. W.E. Ladd.

Besides being home to local residents, Halifax was the base for over 5000 soldiers and sailors, 600 of whom were medical personnel. They were quickly mobilized by their commanding officers to assist with disaster relief of all kinds. Within minutes, boats were dispatched from HMS *Changuinola* at her Dockyard anchorage. Rescuers were overwhelmed by the devastation and the extent of the fires, but nevertheless managed to get many of the injured to the waterfront where they were transported to hospitals or taken by tug or cutter to ships with medical personnel.

Commander John Hopkyns of HMS *Highflyer* spent most of the day directing naval personnel in house-to-house searches for survivors. They set up temporary first-aid stations on shore where they began treating injured children. USS *Old Colony* was turned into a hospital and its crew was organized into search parties. Most of the injured from the ships and along the waterfront were taken aboard *Old Colony.*

The stubborn fires prevented providing medical assistance to more of the wounded. Despite the efforts of the longshoremen to secure *Picton*'s cargo of munition, the explosion

Top: Barrington Street near Rector Street. Many railway workers lived in this neighbourhood just west of the rail yards. Africville was located on the other side of the distant hill.

Left: Houses in Dartmouth, which was not as hard hit as Halifax. Almost 100 residents died in the Explosion but many homes and businesses were damaged.

Service vehicles were supplemented by dozens of private cars and trucks commandeered by the Relief Committee to transport the injured to hospitals and to move the homeless to shelters.

Right: Coffins stacked outside Snow and Co. (second building from right) and the Victoria School of Art and Design (far right) located at the corner of Argyle and Carmichael Streets.

No. 2 Dressing Station was listed as being located at the corner of Oxford, Charles and Chebucto. Most of the injuries caused by the explosion were treated in various dressing stations and clinics located throughout Halifax and Dartmouth. Only a quarter of the 8000 injured received hospital attention.

created fires on *Picton* and on the tug *Musquash*, which also carried ammunition. Naval personnel were diverted from their humanitarian work to fight fires because more than 200 of the port's 500 longshoremen were either killed or badly injured by the Explosion.

Shortly after 1000, word spread that the magazine at Wellington Barracks, located south of Pier 6, was on fire and that it could explode at any time. Rumours that an evacuation order had been issued for the North End resulted in long lines of quiet, calm, able-bodied and injured men, women

and children streaming south towards the Commons, the Citadel and Point Pleasant Park. It was never determined who had raised the alarm; the magazine was never in danger of exploding thanks to the quick thinking of some soldiers who managed to quickly put out a number of small fires. It has been suggested that white steam emanating from the barracks was mistaken for smoke. As a result, nearly two hours of rescue time was lost until an all-clear signal sent people rushing back. Many brave people, especially medical personnel, had ignored the evacuation rumour and remained to fight fires,

American Red Cross personnel at St. Mary's College, Windsor Street.

attempt rescues and provide medical assistance.

Most initial medical treatments were provided by mothers who bandaged their children with torn sheets or by teachers who treated horrendous gashes from glass or lacerations caused by splinters of wood. There were many stories of a parent in shock clinging to a child, long bereft of life, while waiting patiently at a doctor's office or hospital, hoping for a miracle. Medical personnel who were not on duty at the time of the Explosion spent the first hours in their homes treating the wounded who had been brought to them.

By noon the Halifax Relief Committee had been estab- lished to oversee all aspects of the emergency. Chaired by a former mayor, Robert MacIlreith, more than a dozen different committees were formed and quickly went about their work. Private automobiles, trucks, military vehicles, cabs and deliv- ery wagons were all commandeered by the Transportation Committee to pick up the dead and injured. In transit, med- ical personnel would check for signs of life among those being transported to hospitals, and the dead were often removed from the car or wagon to make room for the living.

Most of the hospitals had been damaged by the Explosion and nearly all had their windows broken. Military

Alexander McKay School was built in 1916 to accommodate the growing student population of the north end. It survived the explosion with only minor damage and was used for a while for rescue and reconstruction efforts before returning to its use as a school. It is now the Shambhala School.

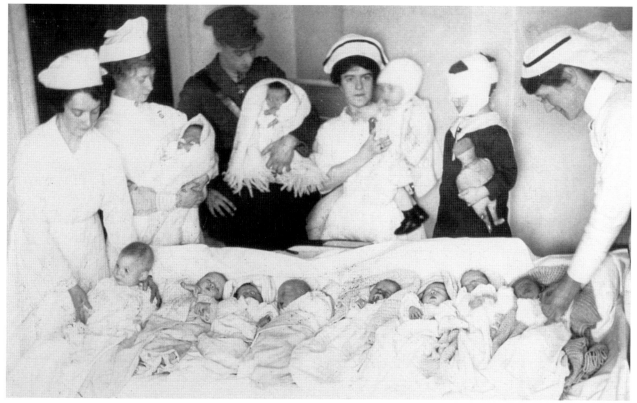

YMCA Emergency Hospital; many children were orphaned by the explosion, discovered in wrecked homes throughout the North End.

personnel under the direction of medical officers and nurses boarded up broken windows and holes in walls. They also set up cots and helped make room on floors and in hallways for the mattresses needed for the large numbers of patients. Camp Hill Hospital had only 250 beds, yet it admitted 1400 patients on the first day. The Dockyard hospital, located at Admiralty House, began treating victims immediately after the Explosion.

By 2100, army engineers and ordnance personnel had erected a canvas hospital on the Commons complete with floors, beds, blankets and stoves which could accommodate over 200 patients. The YMCA had been fully stocked as a dressing station and other hospitals were established at the Halifax Academy of Music and at numerous other schools

and halls. Volunteers combed the North End looking for survivors and brought those who were now homeless to various shelters.

By noon, a train that had arrived in Rockingham shortly

The Harvard University medical team at the American relief hospital.

St. Joseph's Roman Catholic Church after the explosion. The stained glass window tells the stories of the parishoners' experiences after the Explosion.

after the Explosion departed for Truro with some survivors. Soon after, another arrived from Kentville with medical personnel and other volunteers. A train from Pictou County brought more medical personnel and supplies and returned to New Glasgow with patients for the Aberdeen Hospital.

A relief committee was established in Boston by the State of Massachusetts and the American Red Cross to organize a relief train for Halifax. At 2200 on December 6, a train left Boston with twelve surgeons, ten nurses and enough furnishings and supplies for a "completely furnished war hospital." It arrived in Halifax on the afternoon of the eighth and a hospital was established at Bellevue, on Spring Garden Road. A second train from Boston arrived on the ninth and established a hospital at Saint Mary's College on Windsor Street. Medical contingents also arrived from Rhode Island and Maine.

The local doctors, with the help of others from around the province, had the situation well in hand by the time the first American contingent arrived, but they were exhausted. In the days that followed, the work of local civilian and military medical personnel was greatly facilitated by the efforts of the

The Hubley block of houses, closer to the explosion site than St. Joseph's Church and Convent, survived with minimal damage being in the lee of Fort Needham.

Waiting for food rations at the Armouries.

American doctors and nurses and the contribution of the much-needed medical supplies and equipment. Most of the life-threatening injuries were attended to within the first 48 hours after the Explosion, leaving a host of eye operations or removals to be performed, and the setting of numerous compound fractures. Nearly 600 survivors sustained eye injuries, with many losing one eye, and 16 people losing both eyes. Nearly 40 survivors were left totally blinded.

The St. John's Ambulance Brigade, the Victorian Order of Nurses and the nurses of the Red Cross voluntary aid department visited the devastated area, treating those with minor injuries in their homes or in one of over 15 dressing stations located throughout Halifax and Dartmouth. Of the 8000 injured as a result of the explosion, only about 2500 were actually treated in hospitals.

Funds for relief supplies and temporary housing later came as financial aid worth over $25 million from Canadian governments and from sources throughout the Empire. The Dominion government contributed $18 million; another $5 million came from the British government. The initial American contribution of medical supplies and personnel was later supplemented by an additional $700,000 for building materials, clothing, furniture and other supplies under the auspices of the Massachusetts-Halifax Relief Fund. Newspapers of the day also reported hundreds of donations of money, clothing and food items from individuals and organizations all over

Children were often the only able-bodied members of a family available to pick up relief supplies from the various depots located around the city.

North America and Europe. By early 1918, over $23 million had been donated for relief and reconstruction.

Although British and American sailors and Canadian soldiers continued to search through the wreckage for survivors well into the evening of December 6, for most, the fires had taken their toll. Just before noon on the seventh, new difficul-

ties arose when it began to snow. A company of Canadian soldiers began searching through some ruined buildings on Barrington Street at the corner of Kenny, also known as the Flynn Block. Private Benjamin Henneberry had rescued his wife and two of his children from the wreckage on the previous day and was glad to have an opportunity to search for his

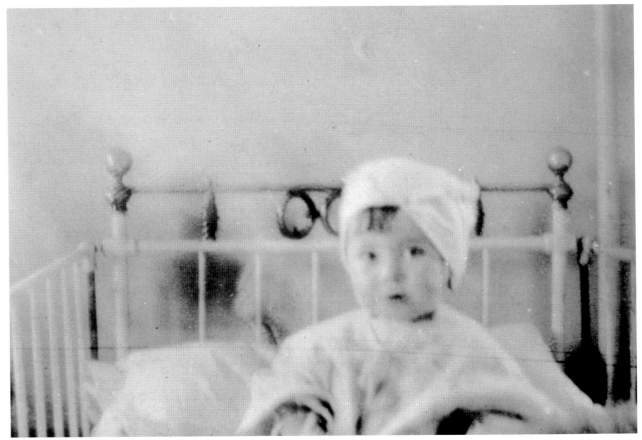

Annie Liggins was discovered in the wreckage of a home more than 24 hours after the Explosion, having been protected from the weather by the ash pan of a stove. One of the soldiers who found her gave her this photo with a note on the back: "Annie Liggins. (ashpan baby). Rescued after being buried for 26 hr [sic] under debris of house. Compliments of Co. Sgt Major Davies. Machine Gunner. 63rd. H.R." Annie's mother and brother perished. She was later reunited with her father upon his return from the war in France.

five other children, who were still missing.

Hearing a faint sound from the cellar, the rescuers found a two-year-old girl under a still-warm stove, protected from the cold by the ash pan. She was taken to the hospital at Pine Hill where she was tentatively identified as a Henneberry child. The child was later identified as Annie Liggins, whose family had lived in a neighbouring apartment. Her discovery gave hope that others might be found. Stories such of this were very rare, however, and as the snow increased and the temperature dropped, all hope of finding more survivors faded.

As the raging snowstorm continued on December 7 and 8, dumping over 40 centimetres of snow on the city, emphasis shifted to providing for the survivors. Whether still in their homes, in shelters or in hospitals, adequate food, clothing and heating fuel were needed. Volunteers delivered these necessities of life to many of those who remained in their damaged, windowless homes, while others were directed to distribution points located throughout Halifax and Dartmouth. When the weather moderated on the ninth, the snow turned into a torrent of black slush. This was followed by more snow and another cold snap which coated the ruined buildings with a layer of ice and endangered their exposed inhabitants.

Of the most important and grim duties of the Relief

Staff of the YMCA Emergency Hospital.

Committee was the work of the Mortuary Committee, chaired by Arthur Barnstead. By the evening of the December 6, Chebucto Road School was selected to house the morgue. The basement was cleared and the lights which had been shattered by the blast were replaced. By night, troops delivered bodies to the morgue from the hospitals and from the undertakers. Local embalmers were joined by others from around the province and from as far away as Montreal. Each body was numbered and identified by written descriptions including sex, approximate age, any distinguishing marks, clothing, personal effects, and the location where the body was found. Most of the clothes were destroyed but other personal effects were placed in a small linen bag, closed with a

drawstring. On this was attached a tag on which the mortuary number was noted.

For nearly a month, crowds of people came to the morgue seeking family members or friends. Before being taken to the basement to view the bodies, each person was interviewed and the information provided was compared to the numbered list and descriptions. The names of those identifying bodies were added to the mortuary records before the bodies were released for burial. In most instances, visual identification was possible. In cases of serious disfigurement or missing limbs, descriptions of the clothing or personal possessions were relied upon. In many instances, victims were identified by a spouse, parent, sibling or close relative, or in the case of a ship's crew, the captain or master of the vessel. Captain E. Peck of the British registered merchant ship *Curaca* was called upon to identify most of the nearly 50 members of his crew who were killed.

In many of the homes close to the Explosion, everyone was killed. Since many members of an extended family lived in close proximity to each other, it was not uncommon to have a death toll of up to ten people for a particular family group. In the extended family of James Jackson and Elizabeth O'Halloran, 46 of the 66 who were in Richmond on December 6 perished within a three-block area. Another 19 were injured and only one was unharmed.

By Christmas, most of the survivors who could not feasibly remain in their own homes were provided with shelter at various locations throughout the city. Service organizations provided gifts and treats for the children, especially those who had been orphaned. For many survivors Christmas would never be the same. Instead of being an occasion of joy and happiness it was to become a reminder of tragedy and loss. Yet, as the new year dawned, recovery gave way to reconstruction, of both the devastated cities and of the lives of the survivors.

Children's Christmas party at the Knights of Columbus Hall. Relief Committee personnel and volunteers made every effort to make Christmas something special for young survivors. The girl with bandages on her face is Minnie (Mary) Anderson. She suffered cuts and eye injuries from shattering glass in the cloakroom of St. Joseph's Girls School. A doctor recommended the removal of her eyes but her father convinced him otherwise. Mary and her family remained at the Knights of Columbus Hall until the temporary buildings on the Exhibition Ground were completed.

5

RECRIMINATION AND RECONSTRUCTION

For those who could see the burning *Mont-Blanc*, the cause of the explosion was obvious. Others thought that the city had been attacked by German aircraft or ships. One man watching the cloud of billowing smoke after the blast swore he saw a German zeppelin flying over the city.

From early in the war, German-born Canadians were required to report to authorities on a regular basis. After the Explosion, those living in Halifax were taken into custody. In the days that followed, rumours frequently held that German spies had sabotaged *Mont-Blanc,* aided and abetted by mem-

The east slope of Fort Needham after much of the debris had been cleaned up.

Temporary housing, Bell Road.

informed them that he had, in fact, survived.

Much of the blame also focused on the crew of *Mont-Blanc,* who were accused of cowardice in not trying to extinguish the fire and in fleeing before issuing a proper warning of the ship's volatile cargo. It was suggested that *Mont-Blanc* should have been flying a red flag to indicate that she was carrying explosives, even though marine regulations only required a vessel to do this while loading or discharging cargo, not while underway. The public outcry was so intense that Le Médec requested, and was given, police protection for himself and his crew for their entire stay in Halifax. Despite the suspicion and innuendo, much of what was raised during the cross-examination of witnesses at the subsequent inquiry was unsubstantiated; there is no evidence that the collision was deliberate or that it was caused by subversive operatives in Halifax on board either vessel, or both. It would not be surprising, however, if there had been German spies in Halifax during the First World War and if they had been providing important intelligence on

bers of the German-born population of Halifax. Anyone who spoke a foreign language became suspect. To some, Norwegian sounded enough like German to lead to the accusation of members of *Imo*'s crew of trying to communicate with German operatives from their hospital beds. Swede Gustav Aström, one of *Imo*'s stokers, recounted that he and his shipmates, especially *Imo*'s helmsman, Johan Johansen, feared for their lives and were relieved when an armed guard was mounted at their hospital. Anström's family in Sweden thought he had perished in the blast and they held a funeral for him and even read his will. When he arrived in New York, nearly two months after the explosion, he

Crew of Mont-Blanc. *Only one crew member, a gunner, died as a result of the explosion. The surviving crew were detained pending the inquiry.*

ship movements. That these activities in any way led to the disaster is totally unfounded.

Even if it were not the fault of the Germans or the French, blame – or at least responsibility – for the accident lay with someone. Within a week of the Explosion, the Department of Marine established a commission of inquiry before the Wreck Commissioner's Court, presided over by Justice Arthur Drysdale, a Nova Scotia admiralty judge of the Exchequer Court of Canada. Assisting him as nautical assessors were Captain Walter Hose, RCN, and Captain Louis Auguste Demers, the Dominion wreck commissioner. Such an inquiry was routine, under the Canada Shipping Act, in cases of loss or damage to vessels or other marine facilities.

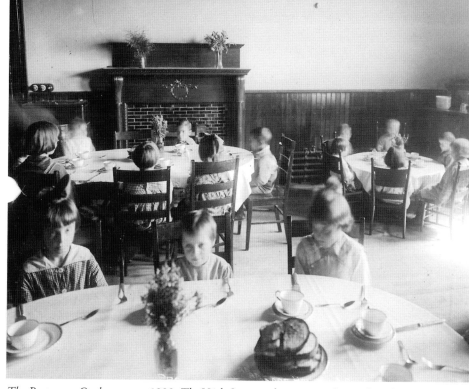

The Protestant Orphanage, c. 1922. The Veith Street orphanage was destroyed in the Explosion and temporary accommodation was provided by the Royal Nova Scotia Yacht Squadron near Point Pleasant Park, until a new facility was built.

Besides the crown counsel, there were five other lawyers, representing the attorney general of Nova Scotia, the City of Halifax, the Halifax Pilotage Commission and the companies which owned the two vessels. Since such proceedings could result in subsequent criminal or civil litigation, the inquiry was conducted much like a trial with each of the lawyers having an opportunity to cross-examine witnesses, which they did with vigour. Charles Burchell, the lawyer for the South Pacific Whaling Company, the owners of *Imo*, was especially aggressive, insinuating all sorts of scenarios when cross-examining naval officials and the pilot and captain of *Mont-Blanc*. Each day the newspapers carried detailed accounts of the proceedings, which only served to incite public condemnation of those responsible for the operation of the port and the vessels involved. The crew of *Mont-Blanc* were an easy target since their vessel was the

one which was carrying the explosives and they all, save one, had survived.

The court sat for 19 days between December 13 and January 29 and heard testimony from 61 witnesses. Justice Drysdale's decision, handed down on February 4, found the pilot and captain of *Mont-Blanc* solely responsible for the collision. He recommended that both be relieved of their duties and that the Chief Examining Officer, Commander Frederick Wyatt, was guilty of neglect of his duties. He also assigned lesser blame to Edward Renner, the pilot of *Clara,* which had preceded *Mont-Blanc* up the harbour, and to the pilotage service in general. Mackey, Le Médec and Wyatt were arrested and charged with manslaughter in the deaths of Captain From and Pilot Hayes of *Imo*. The charges were later dismissed for lack of evidence.

Top: The completed Hydrostone district in 1921 as seen looking to the northwest from the top of Fort Needham.

Left: One of the houses built on Albert Street by the Halifax Relief Commission. Many houses like this one have been renovated and have proven to be well built homes.

Above: This Albert Street house was wood frame construction with framed stucco on the exterior of the second story.

When the owners of both vessels each sued the other in the Nova Scotia division of the Exchequer Court of Canada for $2 million for damages and costs arising out of the collision and explosion, the case was heard by Justice Drysdale. His decision in this instance, not surprisingly, was to again find the captain and pilot of *Mont-Blanc* solely to blame because he found their vessel to be in the wrong channel. The owners of *Mont-Blanc* appealed this decision at the Supreme

Governor Samuel W. McCall of Massachusetts initiated the relief efforts from New England. Workers built 40 eight-unit, two-storey buildings on the Exhibition Grounds in two months.

cerned with basic necessities like food, shelter and clothing. Although the Halifax Relief Committee, through the work of its various sub-committees, had done a good job of providing for the immediate needs of those affected by the disaster, a more permanent administrative structure was required to oversee the long-term rehabilitation and reconstruction of the devastated area. On January 22, 1918, the Dominion government established the Halifax Relief

Court of Canada, which, on a vote of three to two, found both ships equally to blame for the accident. Both parties made a further appeal to the Privy Council in London, which upheld the Supreme Court decision that both vessels were at fault and thus both shared responsibility for the collision.

Ultimately, Francis Mackey was reinstated as a harbour pilot, later retiring after many years of service. He always maintained that *Imo* was at fault because she had left her anchorage without permission. Captain Le Médec was sent to New York and returned to sea the following summer. He retired in 1932 after 26 years of service with la Compagnie Générale Transatlantique. Commander Wyatt received an administrative discharge from the RCN and moved to the United States.

Imo remained ashore in Dartmouth until late April 1918 when she was refloated. After minor repairs she was sent to New York to be fitted out as a whale factory ship. She was sold in 1920 and renamed *Guvernoren*. In 1921, less than a week before the fourth anniversary of the Explosion, she ran aground near Port Stanley, Falkland Islands, and was abandoned.

While some Haligonians followed the Wreck Commissioner's inquiry with interest, most were more con-

Commission, chaired by Halifax lawyer T. Sherman Rogers, to take over the work of the Relief Committee. Its duties involved the administrating the Relief Committee funds and recommending ways of "restoring or assisting in the restoration of the area affected."

Each of the relief sub-committees submitted reports to the commission outlining their activities during the six weeks since the explosion. These duties, whether dealing with the long and short-term needs of survivors, or the rehabilitation of Halifax's North End, now became the responsibility of the commission.

Workers had already begun to repair damaged homes so that people could be moved from the temporary shelters. Labourers and teamsters were hired from as far away as Montreal to clear the devastated area of debris, permitting tradesmen to begin the work of repairing existing buildings and building much-needed temporary accommodations.

Although many homes had been repaired and made liveable by late January, it was estimated that accommodations for nearly 5000 survivors were still required. Colonel Robert Low was sent to Halifax by the Dominion government to oversee the work of the reconstruction committee. Low had extensive experience at designing and building military camps

The children are residents of the buildings and the baby in the carriage (supplied by the Massachusetts-Halifax Relief Committee) is Charles Vaughan, a future mayor of Halifax. Adults from left to right: Mr. Harrigan, the governor's bodyguard; Gov. Samuel W. McCall; G. Fred Pearson; Capt. Hathaway, the governor's aide-de-camp; the chauffeur; Ralph P. Bell, secretary of the Halifax Relief Commission; Dr. G.B. Cullen (November 8, 1918).

during the early years of the First World War. His job was to build 832 self-contained housing units on three sites in Halifax: at the former Exhibition Grounds on Almon Street, at the Garrison Grounds off Sackville Street, on the South Common along Bell Road, and near Victoria Park in Dartmouth. The units were completed and ready for occupancy in March 1918, by which time the Commission had also completed 3000 repair orders for damaged houses.

The temporary buildings were built of wood and Beaverboard and were equipped with water, electricity and sewage. Monthly rents ranged from five dollars per month for

two rooms to twelve dollars for four rooms and bath. For many occupants it was actually an improvement in their living conditions prior to December 6. The apartments, designed to last for five years — were mostly furnished in less than three months, and provided warm, secure, spacious accommodation. The Massachusetts-Halifax Relief Fund provided the furnishings which included everything from furniture to linens and cutlery. Eligible families chose from among a variety of styles of furniture which they were to keep even when they moved out of the temporary buildings. The Relief Fund considered this a gift to the people of Halifax

Massachusetts-Halifax Relief Committee warehouse, Windsor Street. The Massachusetts Relief Fund distributed over $750,000 worth of assistance, including the furnishings for the temporary housing.

from the people of Massachusetts.

The commission paid out claims for property losses, both residential and commercial. Applicants could be eligible for compensation for personal losses, such as for the cost of lost or ruined clothing. Store owners could claim for lost merchandise and for the cost of starting up a new business. Each claim for property compensation was based on its own merits and was heard in court, presided over by lawyers. Decisions were made at the hearing and payments were usually made the same day.

The commission also established a pension plan for sur-

vivors who had suffered permanent disabilities and for those whose injuries prevented them from earning a living. Amputees and those who were blinded were provided with special assistance, many receiving modest pensions for the rest of their lives. Child-care allowances were provided for widows so they could find employment. The pensions were meant to supplement the income of the recipients and to encourage them to become more self-sufficient. A widow's pension, for example, amounted to about one-third of the family's monthly income before the Explosion, to a maximum of $65 per month.

Aerial view of the Hydrostone district. Over the years the growth of trees and gardens in the Hydrostone district have fulfilled the promise of proponents of the Garden City movement.

Temporary housing on Exhibition Grounds (top) and workers' housing at Young Street and Kempt Road (left). The Young Street area was named "Cavicchiville" after the general contractor for the project Cavicchi and Paligano.

Temporary housing, Garrison Grounds.

Below: Buildings under construction on the south side of Columbus Place, July 30, 1919. Note the different designs incorporated in the development. The house at far right was built at the west end of the boulevard to provide a break with the older housing further to the west. Each of the boulevards originally had a house in this location, but they were later demolished.

By the time the Relief Commission was disbanded in 1976, there were still 66 pensioners on the books. The monthly payments had increased over 58 years. They ranged from monthly installments of roughly $200 for a widow's pension to over $400 for a man who had been blinded. By 1989, approximately half this number were receiving pensions through the Department of Veterans Affairs who were administering the fund then estimated to be worth $800,000.

The temporary apartments were a stop-gap solution and the commission still had to decide how to provide permanent homes for the homeless. Instead of rebuilding houses on their original sites, it was decided to produce a coherent community plan for the new development. In 1918, one of the innovative approaches to urban planning was the Garden City movement. The late nineteenth century British envi-

Hydrostone manufacturing facility located in Eastern Passage, near natural supplies of beach and sand. Work was well underway by the time this photo was taken in August 1919.

Thomas Adams, a leading figure in the Garden City movement.

These three wood frame houses on Robie Street were built for the Halifax Housing Commission in an area formerly known as "Hennessey Field."

ronmental reform movement was characterized by grouping self-contained communities interspersed with abundant green spaces to promote healthy living and socialization in a half-industrial, half-agricultural milieu.

The leading proponent of garden city planning in Canada was Thomas Adams. He had moved to Canada from Britain where he had been instrumental in developing the new town of Letchworth, a model for garden city development in Britain and North America. Canadian cities had experienced a period of uncontrolled growth due to the industrialization of the late nineteenth century and were ready for the use of

imaginative urban planning. Halifax's North End seemed to be an ideal spot for this type of orderly development. Because the area had been so totally devastated, reconstruction offered an opportunity not only to provide modern housing, but to also apply modern architectural and urban planning principles in the redesign of an old community.

The proposal was focused on nine hectares west of Fort Needham, in an area known as Merkelsfield, bounded by Young, Isleville, Duffus and Gottingen streets. It would involve the expropriation of over 100 parcels of land and when completed would provide 326 dwellings in 88 build-

Halifax Housing Commission houses on Robie Street, 2004.

ings. The south end of the development on Young Street consisted of a city block of 18 shops and offices. Eight of the nine one-block streets contained landscaped, treed boulevards with service lanes between the yards of adjoining streets. This design served to provide an ambiance suited to the principles of the Garden City movement.

The commission's plan was not met with immediate approval by North End residents. Many wanted the houses rebuilt on their original lots and streets. They had owned their homes and were not interested in becoming tenants. Despite the opposition, the proposal developed by Adams, in association with architect George Ross of the Montreal firm Ross and MacDonald, was approved, with construction commencing in September 1918, nine months after the Explosion.

A manufacturing plant was built in Eastern Passage, close to natural supplies of clean gravel and sand. This facility produced the patented, fire-resistant concrete blocks known as Hydrostone. The 9 x 24-inch (23 x 61-cm) blocks were moulded under pressure and steam-cured to allow for slow evaporation. The plant was able to produce up to 4000 blocks per day. The completed blocks were transported to a dock on a narrow gauge railway, then taken by barge to a rail siding in North End Halifax, where they were again loaded onto rail cars and transported to the construction sites. By using the Hydrostone blocks construction costs were kept lower than when building brick houses, and no formwork was required for the walls.

The new houses were completed over a period of two years, with the first units being occupied in March 1919. They were constructed in six different designs, ranging in size from four-and-a-half to seven rooms. The streets were named after famous explorers or local merchants and, although different names were considered for the area, it became generally

Houses on Albert Street c. 1924 (above), 2004 (below).

North end streetscapes reflect houses built before, immediately after and during the 85 years following the explosion.

known as "the Hydrostone."

As survivors of the Explosion, the initial tenants had an unusually strong community bond. Many families remained in the Hydrostone for generations, and when the Relief Commission put the houses up for sale in 1949 they became North End homeowners once again.

In an effort to help "seed" the rest of the North End for additional development, Ross and MacDonald also designed over 200 other houses outside the Hydrostone, some for individual owners and others for the Halifax Housing Commission. Most of these were built of wood, a less expensive material in the construction of individual buildings.

Despite these new developments, the North End did not experience the type of growth expected in 1918. During the Depression many homes in the Hydrostone lay empty. Even at the modest rents charged, they were too expensive for families with no jobs and only minimal income. The next housing boom in the North End did not occur until the Second

This row of shops at the south end of the Hydrostone district continue to be used for a variety of services for local residents. The building in the foreground was the office of the Halifax Relief Commission from 1921 until the early 1980s.

Halifax's North End, 2004.

and rail line in the South End was completed a few years later. The Halifax Shipyard emerged bigger than ever.

Other institutions were also transformed. The new Richmond School opened in 1921, part of the new Adams-inspired square on Dartmouth Avenue at Devonshire Avenue, one of the new diagonal streets linking Barrington Street to Gottingen Street. St. Joseph's School was rebuilt on the site of the one destroyed by the Explosion.

A new St. Joseph's Church opened in 1920 as a temporary basement church, a foundation for a future, more elaborate place of worship. It would take nearly 40 years until the larger permanent church was built on top of the foundation. A new St. Mark's Church was also built. The congregations of Kaye Street Methodist and Grove Presbyterian churches also built a temporary church, known as the "tar paper" church, at the corner of Young and Gottingen streets. These two congregations eventually united and, together built the United Memorial Church which was dedicated on September 18, 1921. Barbara Orr presented the church with a chime of bronze bells in memory of her parents and five siblings.

In Dartmouth, four churches — Emmanuel Anglican, Grace Methodist, Stairs Memorial Presbyterian and Dartmouth Baptist churches were rebuilt. A new Park School was built to accommodate the students of Central and Park schools, as those schools were damaged beyond repair. Tufts Cove School was rebuilt, but the Mi'kmaq school at Tufts Cove was not rebuilt as the reserve was abandoned.

World War when the "pre-fab" became the house of choice. Built to meet the burgeoning wartime population, these homes seemed to spring up throughout the north and west ends of the city. Like the houses built after the Explosion, these relatively inexpensive and well-built structures provided and continue to provide homes for the people of Halifax.

The North End's industrial base never regained the prominence it had prior to December 1917. Of the four Richmond piers, only Pier 9 was rebuilt and expanded. The Hillis & Sons Foundry was rebuilt, not on the same site, but further north on Kempt Road. Oland Brewery on Agricola Street was rebuilt, while the nearby site of the cotton mill was replaced by a building supply company. In Dartmouth, Crathorne's Mill and Halifax Brewery were not rebuilt. Although it was badly damaged, Consumer Cordage was repaired. North Street Station was repaired and in use until the new station

6

LEGACY

For most survivors, the memories still spark emotions of sadness and loss. Loss of a parent or sibling, a favourite aunt or uncle, or a best friend: all such recollections are etched in memories by the suddenness and shock of the event. One survivor used to say that on most days he couldn't remember what he had for breakfast but he could *always* remember every minute of "that day." A woman in her late eighties thinks of "that day" every time she washes her face and rubs a wash cloth over scars that caused her more emotional than physical pain in life. The siren of a fire engine causes a man in his eighties to move away from a window and arouses no curiosity about its cause. A great-grandmother still finds that Christmas leaves her with a sense of loss over the disappearance of her best childhood friend with whom she used to imagine what they would become when they "grew up." Another woman mourns the death of an aunt who died before she could complete making her a new coat.

Today's media provide instant and graphic accounts of war zones, man-made catastrophes and natural disasters. In 1917, when news travelled at a much slower pace, Canadians were slow to learn about the worst single disaster in the country's history. Despite the magnitude of the Halifax Explosion, this event was never recognized as part of Canada's sacrifice in the First World War. European placenames, such as Vimy Ridge, Ypres and Passchendaele, have been memorialized for the thousands of Canadian lives lost and thus important to Canada's coming-of-age as a nation.

Today, in Halifax, there are numerous opportunities to learn about the Explosion and its significance. Countless people, places and things offer the chance to reflect. In December 2004, the youngest survivor of the disaster will be 87 years old. Anyone who was old

The Halifax Explosion Memorial Bell Tower located on Fort Needham was inaugurated in June 1985 in memory of all those who suffered because of the blast. It overlooks the site of the Explosion and the area destroyed by the blast.

The mortuary bags contained possessions of unclaimed victims. These were from seven-year-old James Fraser, whose three younger siblings also died. The fate of their mother was not known or recorded. Their father was serving overseas.

challenge us to consider the lives of their owners, whose lives were suddenly cut short by a consequence of war. Unlike the television images of today, the photographs and the locations of the Explosion and its aftermath provide clues to the memories, often not spoken, which bind the survivors together in a manner similar to those D-Day veterans who periodically return to the Normandy coast so they will not forget.

A walk through North End Halifax reveals numerous reminders of the disaster, whether it is a building which survived the blast or a memorial to firemen who lost their lives while doing their job.

Elsewhere, a stained-glass window invites quiet contemplation of the lives of children who died while kneeling in prayer. At another memorial, bells ring out in memory of not just the family whose death inspired their creation, but for the other nearly 2000 souls, many of whom left no one to mourn.

enough to remember the circumstances surrounding the event would be in their early nineties.

Luckily, the accounts of many survivors have been chronicled in books such as *Survivors* and Janet Kitz's *Shattered City*. Radio and television clips in the archives of the CBC document these accounts. Playwrights and songwriters have also tried to reflect these memories in word and song. And, of course, the memories are preserved in the stories passed down through generations within families of survivors.

The collected personal possessions of everyday people — a comb, bus ticket, pencil, marble, school bag or locket —

Although the Explosion was a consequence of war and its victims were similar to those who lived in towns in France and Belgium, Halifax, because it was a military centre, was better equipped to handle the situation. It has been shown that the military assistance in searching for survivors and treating them was responsible for the survival of much of the

Names boards, probably from one of Mont-Blanc's *lifeboats, showing an earlier port of registry - Rouen. These were discovered on the Halifax waterfront near the foot of Morris Street on December 26, 1917.*

The possessions found on a headless male corpse. It is possible that he worked on the waterfront and was a Roman Catholic.

city's subsequent growth and infrastructure.

The shipping containers which move through the port in the twenty-first century are clearly marked with symbols and manifests, listing their contents. Nevertheless, dangerous cargoes are not uncommon and although there will never be a shipment of volatile munitions and explosives as in the case of *Mont-Blanc*, accidents and premeditated acts of sabotage led to similar disasters.

The Halifax Explosion has been the focus of study for those involved in preventing such accidents from

occurring and in reacting to disasters. When compared with modern strategies developed for disaster response, the Halifax experience in 1917 was calm and well organized. The war effort that brought *Mont-Blanc* to

This cup was one of the few intact objects recovered from the Swetnam family home on East Young Street. It was cherished by Dorothy Swetnam Hare whose mother and brother died when the house collapsed and burned.

This house was built prior to the explosion and, although badly damaged, it was repaired and survived to the present day.

the port brought the thousands of military personnel to the city and provided the potential for its salvation. The fact that there was such a large military presence, whose job it was to respond to war-like situations, contributed greatly to the immediate recovery efforts. But it was the efforts of survivors in rescuing and providing immediate care for their loved ones and those around them which contributed most to the recovery efforts. People helping people, neighbours caring for neighbours, this is probably the lasting legacy of the disaster. This and the fading memories of the core of survivors who gather each December 6 to remember and to mourn.

MAP OF SITES IN HALIFAX AND DARTMOUTH RELEVANT TO THE HALIFAX HARBOUR EXPLOSION

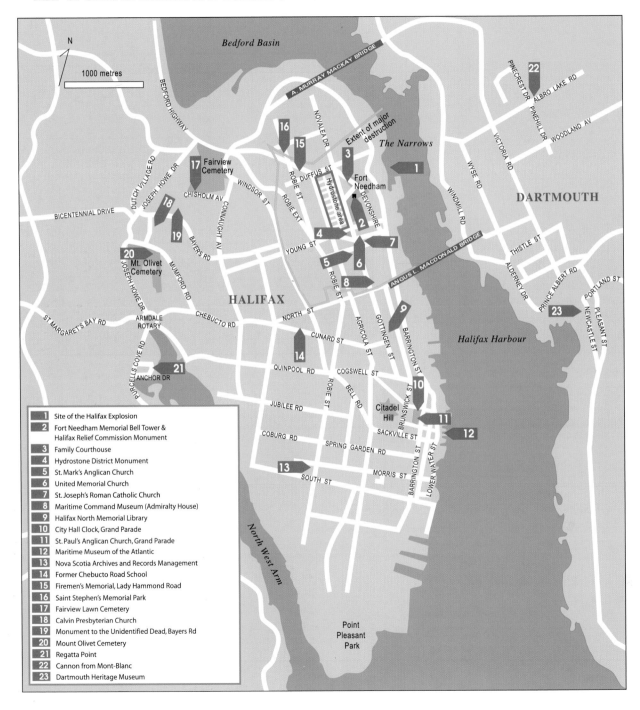

N

1000 metres

Bedford Basin

A. MURRAY MACKAY BRIDGE

The Narrows

Fort Needham

DARTMOUTH

Fairview Cemetery

Hydrostone area

Extent of major destruction

HALIFAX

ANGUS L. MACDONALD BRIDGE

Halifax Harbour

Mt. Olivet Cemetery

ARMDALE ROTARY

Citadel Hill

North West Arm

Point Pleasant Park

1	Site of the Halifax Explosion
2	Fort Needham Memorial Bell Tower & Halifax Relief Commission Monument
3	Family Courthouse
4	Hydrostone District Monument
5	St. Mark's Anglican Church
6	United Memorial Church
7	St. Joseph's Roman Catholic Church
8	Maritime Command Museum (Admiralty House)
9	Halifax North Memorial Library
10	City Hall Clock, Grand Parade
11	St. Paul's Anglican Church, Grand Parade
12	Maritime Museum of the Atlantic
13	Nova Scotia Archives and Records Management
14	Former Chebucto Road School
15	Firemen's Memorial, Lady Hammond Road
16	Saint Stephen's Memorial Park
17	Fairview Lawn Cemetery
18	Calvin Presbyterian Church
19	Monument to the Unidentified Dead, Bayers Rd
20	Mount Olivet Cemetery
21	Regatta Point
22	Cannon from Mont-Blanc
23	Dartmouth Heritage Museum

EXPLOSION SITES

THESE SITES are significant to the history of the 1917 explosion in Halifax Harbour. The map, opposite, locates them in the city.

1 SITE OF THE HALIFAX EXPLOSION

Pier 6 was never rebuilt and its site is now occupied by a floating dock of Halifax Shipyards Limited.

2 HALIFAX EXPLOSION MEMORIAL BELL TOWER AND HALIFAX RELIEF COMMISSION MONUMENT, FORT NEEDHAM MEMORIAL PARK.

Located high on Fort Needham hill, the memorial tower overlooks the site of Pier 6 (#2) where *Mont-Blanc* exploded. The monument was built with private and public donations, many given in memory of victims of the disaster. It houses a carillon of bells which had been donated to United Memorial Church in 1920 by Barbara Orr in memory of her entire family: mother, father, two brothers and three sisters, all of whom perished in the explosion. Four additional bells were added in 1990. The monument was dedicated on June 9, 1985, and every December 6 at 0900, it is the site of a service in memory of victims of the Explosion.

In the same park is the monument recording the names of the Commissioners of the Halifax Relief Committee (1918-50) and a plaque commemorating the establishment of Fort Needham Memorial Park.

3 FAMILY COURTHOUSE, ACADIA STREET

This building was constructed in the early 1920s as Richmond School to replace the original school of that name destroyed in the Explosion. A plaque commemorating the 88 students of Richmond School lost in the disaster is mounted inside the main door. The building currently serves as the Family Courthouse.

4 HYDROSTONE DISTRICT MONUMENT, YOUNG STREET

The Hydrostone area has been designated a National Historic Site. It was built between 1918 and 1921 to provide 326 permanent homes. It is an excellent example of a community designed on the principles of the Garden City movement and was built using a patented type of concrete block, known as hydrostone, after which the district was named.

5 ST. MARK'S ANGLICAN CHURCH, GOTTINGEN STREET

St. Mark's was built in 1920 to replace the original church, which was destroyed in the Explosion.

6 UNITED MEMORIAL CHURCH, KAYE STREET

Dedicated on September 18, 1921, United Memorial was built by the congregations of the former Kaye Street Methodist Church and Grove Presbyterian Church, both of which were destroyed in the Explosion. The joining of congregations took place four years before the establishment of the United Church of Canada. The church's interior displays interesting photographs and memorials relating to the Explosion.

7 ST. JOSEPH'S ROMAN CATHOLIC CHURCH,
RUSSELL STREET

The original building was destroyed in the Explosion and was replaced by a basement church in 1920. The present building was built on top of the basement church in the 1959. The stained glass memorial windows tell the story of the church's parishioners and their experiences at the time of the Explosion.

8 MARITIME COMMAND MUSEUM (ADMIRALTY HOUSE), GOTTINGEN STREET

This building served as the Dockyard hospital following the Explosion. The museum holds photos and documents relating to the navy's role in the disaster.

9 HALIFAX NORTH MEMORIAL LIBRARY,
GOTTINGEN STREET

This library was built with the assistance of the Halifax Relief Commission. Both the building, and the sculpture at its entrance, were built as a memorial to the victims of the Explosion.

10 CITY HALL CLOCK,
GRAND PARADE

The north face of the clock is permanently stopped at 9:05 a.m., the time that the original clock stopped as a result of the Explosion.

11 ST. PAUL'S ANGLICAN CHURCH, GRAND PARADE

An image etched upon one of this church's windows resembles the profile of a late 18th-century church official. Inside the church, a piece of metal from *Mont-Blanc* remains embedded above the door in the inside wall of the porch.

12 MARITIME MUSEUM OF THE ATLANTIC, LOWER WATER STREET

A copy of the *Halifax Explosion Memorial Book* — containing the names of 1953 victims of the Explosion — is on permanent display here. The

exhibit, *Halifax Wrecked,* contains numerous photographs, personal artifacts and pieces of the *Mont-Blanc*. CSS *Acadia* which was in the harbour on December 6, 1917, is permanently docked at the museum.

13 NOVA SCOTIA ARCHIVES AND RECORDS MANAGEMENT, UNIVERSITY AVENUE

The archives house photographs, artifacts, documents, newspapers and books relating to the Explosion, including the corporate records of the Halifax Relief Commission.

14 FORMER CHEBUCTO ROAD SCHOOL, CHEBUCTO ROAD

The basement of this building served as the official mortuary for bodies of victims of the Explosion. Funerals for the unidentified dead were conducted in front of this building, drawing over 300 people.

15 FIREMEN'S MEMORIAL, LADY HAMMOND ROAD

This memorial commemorates nine firemen killed in the Halifax Explosion.

16 ST. STEPHEN'S MEMORIAL PARK, NORMANDY DRIVE

In this small park are a memorial to those who fought in both world wars, a fragment thought to be from *Mont-Blanc* and a fragment from the altar of the original St. Joseph's Church.

17 FAIRVIEW LAWN CEMETERY, WINDSOR STREET

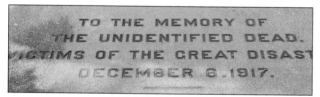

TO THE MEMORY OF THE UNIDENTIFIED DEAD. VICTIMS OF THE GREAT DISAST DECEMBER 6, 1917.

Near the Chisholm Avenue entrance is a monument to the unidentified victims of the disaster. A memorial to 45 crew members of SS *Curaca* and the graves of many other Explosion victims are located here.

18 CALVIN PRESBYTERIAN CHURCH, ASHBURN AVENUE

A piece of the anchor shank from *Mont-Blanc* has been mounted near the spot where it landed.

19 MONUMENT TO THE UNIDENTIFIED DEAD, BAYERS ROAD

Later burials of unidentified victims took place at this site. The monument was once part of Fairview Lawn Cemetery.

20 MOUNT OLIVET CEMETERY, MUMFORD ROAD

A monument at this site is dedicated to the unidentified dead. The graves of Royal Canadian Navy and Royal Navy personnel, and other victims of the Explosion are located here.

21 REGATTA POINT, ANCHOR DRIVE

The anchor shank of *Mont-Blanc*, weighing 502 kg, was hurled by the blast 3.8 km to this site.

22 CANNON FROM MONT-BLANC. CORNER OF ALBRO LAKE ROAD AND PINECREST DRIVE

The cannon is displayed near the spot where it landed nearly three kilometres from the site of the Explosion. The monument lists the names of Dartmouth residents who perished in the Explosion.

23 DARTMOUTH HERITAGE MUSEUM, NEWCASTLE STREET

The museum holds many documents and photographs relating to the effect of the Explosion on the Dartmouth community.

Selected Books and Videos

Non-Fiction

Armstrong, John Griffith *The Halifax Explosion and the Royal Canadian Navy* (Vancouver: University of British Columbia Press, 2002)

Beed, Blair *1917 Explosion and American Response* (Halifax: Dtours Visitor and Convention Service, 1998)

Bird, Michael J. *The Town That Died: A Chronicle of the Halifax Disaster* (Toronto: McGraw-Hill Ryerson Limited, 1962)

Chapman, Harry *Dartmouth's Day of Anguish* (Dartmouth: Dartmouth Museum Society,1992)

Howell, Colin D. and Alan Ruffman, (editors) *Ground Zero: A Reassessment of the 1917 Explosion in Halifax Harbour* (Halifax: Gorsebrook Research Institute, 1994)

Kitz, Janet F. *Shattered City: The Halifax Explosion and the Road to Recovery* (Halifax: Nimbus Publishing Limited, 1989)

Kitz, Janet F. *Survivors: Children of the Halifax Explosion* (Halifax: Nimbus Publishing Limited, 1992)

Mahar, James and Rowena *Too Many to Mourn: One Family's Tragedy* (Halifax: Nimbus Publishing, 1998)

Metson, Graham (ed) *The Halifax Explosion December 6, 1917* (Toronto: McGraw-Hill Ryerson Limited, 1978)

Monnon, Mary Ann *Miracles and Mysteries: The Halifax Explosion December 6, 1917* (Windsor, NS: Lancelot Press, 1977)

Fiction

Barkhouse, Joyce C. *Yesterday's Children* (Windsor, NS: Lancelot Press, 1992)

Lotz, Jim *The Sixth of December* (Markham, ON: Paperjacks Ltd., 1981)

MacNeil, Robert *Burden of Desire* (Toronto, ON: Doubleday Canada Limited, 1992)

MacLennan, Hugh *Barometer Rising* (Toronto, ON: McClelland & Stewart Limited, 1941)

Muir, Paddy *Love from Katie* (Halifax, NS: James-Stonehouse, 1991)

Payzant, Joan M. *Who's A Scaredy-Cat!: A Story of the Halifax Explosion* (Dartmouth, NS: Windmill Press, 1992)

Films/Videos:

City of Ruins: The Halifax Explosion (CBC Home Video, 2004, CHE189103)

"Just One Big Mess" the Halifax Explosion 1917 (National Film Board of Canada, 1993)

Morning of Armageddon (Screen Star Group, SMA Distribution, 1993)

Shattered City (CBC Home Video, 2004, CSC 188103)

Thunder in the Sky (Global Video Inc.,1993)

Photo Credits

Abbreviations: AGNS: Art Gallery of Nova Scotia; Castle/MMA: Materials from the Maritime Museum of the Atlantic Photographed by Gary Castle; CTA: City of Toronto Public Archives; DND/MCE/HSO: Department of National Defence/Hydrographic Services Office; LAC: Library Archives of Canada; MCM: Maritime Command Museum; MMA: Maritime Museum of the Atlantic; NSARM: Nova Scotia Archives and Records Management.

Preliminary Pages: p.4 (top), Len Wagg Photography;p.4 (bottom), MMA/Vaughan Collection, MP207.1.184.86; p.4 (right), DND/MCE/HSO; p.5 LAC.

Chapter 1: pp.7, 8 (top), Private Collection/David B. Flemming; p.8 (bottom), NSARM/Notman Collection, 47-7; p.9, NSARM, Neg. N-0097; p.10 (top), NSARM/Notman Collection, 1983-310/10056; p.10 (bottom), NSARM/Light & Power Collection, ; p.11 (top), MMA, Neg.N-12,877; p.11 (bottom), MCM; p.12 (top), NSARM, Neg. N-744; p.12 (bottom), 13, MCM; p.14 (top), Private Collection/David B. Flemming; p.14 (bottom), MCM; p.15 (top), MMA, MP31.7.45/MP31.7.46; p.15 (bottom), Dalhousie University Art Gallery, *Halifax The First 250 Years*, Formac, 1999.

Chapter 2: pp.16, 17, 18, 19 (right), Private Collection/David B. Flemming; p.19 (left), MMA/Hagen Collection, MP207.1.184.245; p.20, NSARM, Neg. N-6963; p.21 (top), NSARM/NS Supreme Court Collection, 1992-364, Neg. N-7154; p.21 (bottom), MMA, MP207.1.184.244; p.22, AGNS, *The Artists' Halifax*, Formac, 2003; p.23, MMA, MP18.196.1; p.24, MMA, MP23.21.1; p.25, MMA/Slide Collection of the Commission of Inquiry, ; p.26, MMA, MP207.1.184.331; p.27, MMA, MP207.1.184.221; p.28, MMA, MP207.1.184.321; p.29, NSARM; p.30, MMA/Kitz Collection, MP207.1.184.243; p.31, MMA/Kitz Collection, MP207.1.184.242; p.32, MMA, Neg. N–16,274; p.33 (top), LAC, Neg. PA-166585; p.33 (bottom), MMA, Neg. N–16,275; p.34, MMA, MP207.1.184.341; p.35, Gary Castle Photography.

Chapter 3: p.36-7 (bottom), MMA, MP207.1.184, 1a-1d; p.37 (top), MMA, Neg. N–15,067; p.38 (top), MMA, MP207.1.184.38; p.38 (bottom), NSARM,Neg.N-6198; p.39 (bottom), MMA, MP207.1.184.303; p.40 (top), MMA, MP207.1.184.10; p.40 (right), LAC; p.40 (left), MMA, MP207.1.184.344; p.41 (top), MMA/Vaughan Collection, MP207.1.184.78; p.41 (bottom), MMA, MP207.1.184.298; p.42 (top), CTA/William James Collection, #2436; p.42 (bottom), Gary Castle Photography; p.43 (top) MMA/Charles A. Vaughan Collection, MP207.1.184.35; p.43, (bottom), MMA/Castle; p.44 (top), MMA; p.44 (bottom), MMA, MP207.1.184.287; p.45 (top), MMA, M94.5.2; p.45 (bottom), Gary Castle Photography; p.46 (top), MMA, MP207.1.184.218; p.46 (bottom), Gary Castle Photography; p.47, MMA/*40 Views of the Halifax Disaster*, p18; p.48 (top), MMA, MP207.1.184.292; p.48 (bottom), Gary Castle Photography; p.49, MMA, MP207.1.184.46; p.50, MMA, MP207.184.14; p.51, MMA, MP 207.1.184.47; p.52, LAC.

Chapter 4: p.53, MMA, MP207.1.184.61; p.54 (top), NSARM/Halifax Relief Commission, Neg. N-2303; p.54 (bottom), MMA, MP207.1.184.6; p.55, CTA/William James Collection, #1782; p.56 (top), NSARM, Neg. N–201; p.56 (bottom), MMA, MP207.1.184.269; p.57 (top), MMA, MP207.1.184.25; p.57 (bottom), NSARM/Halifax Relief Commission collection, Neg. N-4273; p.58, MMA, MP207.1.184.24; p.59, CTA/William James Collection, #1786; p.60 (top), MMA, MP207.1.184.40; p.60 (bottom), Gary Castle Photography; p.61 (top), MMA, MP207.1.184.217; p.61 (bottom), NSARM/Nathaniel N. Morse Collection, Neg. N-7079; p.62 (top), MMA, MP207.1.184.9a; p.62 (bottom), Private Collection/David B. Flemming; p.63 (top), MMA, MP207.1.184.74; p.63 (bottom), Gary Castle Photography; p.64, NSARM/Nathaniel N. Morse Collection, Neg. N–7082; p.65, NSARM/Halifax Relief Commission Collection, Neg. N–4313; p.66, MMA, MP207.1.184.219; p.67, MMA, MP207.1.184.215; p.68, CTA/William James Collection, #626.

Chapter 5: p.69, MMA, MP207.1.184.149; p.70 (top), MMA, MP207.1.184.94; p.70 (bottom), MMA, MP207.1.184.319; p.71, NSARM/Halifax Relief Commission, N-4840; p.72 (top), MMA, MP207.1.184.130; p.72 (right), Gary Castle Photography; p.72 (left), NSARM/Halifax Relief Commission, MG20,Vol.532, No.2; p.73, MMA/Vaughan Collection, MP205.1.184.104; p.74, MMA/Vaughan Collection, MP207.1.184.106; p.75, NSARM, Neg. N–7012; p.76 (top), NSARM/Halifax Relief Commission, 1976-166.41; p.76 (bottom), Gary Castle Photography; p.77 (top), MMA/Vaughan Collection, p.77 (bottom), MMA, MP207.1.184.100; p.78 (top), MMA, MP207.1.184.95; p.78 (bottom), MMA, MP207.1.184.127; p.79 (top), NSARM/HRC Rehousing, N-7050; p.79 (bottom), NSARM, N-7204; p.80, MMA, MP207.1.184.139; p.81, Gary Castle Photography; p.82 (top), NSARM/Halifax Relief Commission, MG20,Vol.532, No.2; p.82 (bottom), Gary Castle Photography; p.83, Gary Castle Photography; p.84 (top), MMA, MP207.1.184.132; p.84 (bottom), Gary Castle Photography; p.85, Len Wagg Photography.

Chapter 6: p.86, Gary Castle Photography; p.87 (top), MMA, M87.2.192B-b; p.87 (bottom), MMA/Castle; p.88 (top), MMA; p.88 (bottom), Private Collection/David B. Flemming; p.89 (top), MMA, MP207.1.184.134; p.89 (bottom), Gary Castle Photography.

Sites: p.90, Map provided by Peggy McCalla; pp.91-93 Gary Castle Photography.

INDEX